W9-ASU-784

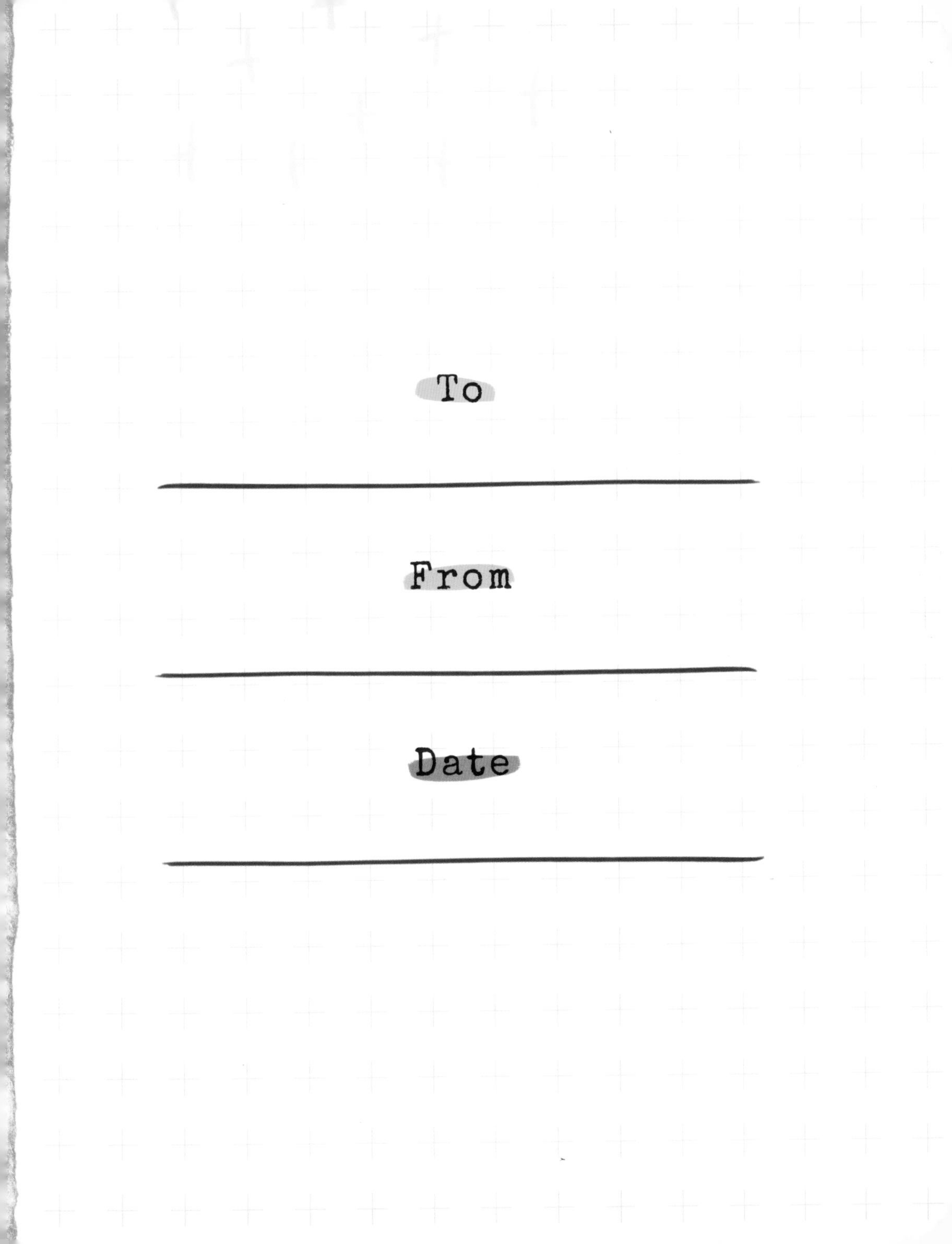
To
From
Date

100 Days of Bible Promises: A Devotional Journal

First Edition, March 2018

Published by:

DaySpring

P.O. Box 1010
Siloam Springs, AR 72761
dayspring.com

Editorial Director: Lisa Stilwell
Art Director: Jessica Wei

Printed in China

Prime: 71925

ISBN: 978-1-68408-216-2

100 days of Bible promises

A Devotional Journal

SHANNA NOEL

HIS GRACE IS SUFFICIENT

Every day, every moment, God reaches into your life with His hand of grace to help you through all that you face. It's His way of saying, "Be assured. I know you are weak, but I am strong. Rest in My power and let My grace take over where your efforts end."

There isn't anything He can't do or accomplish through you, so be glad and rejoice in knowing that wherever you lack, He is more than able!

So let us come boldly to the throne of our gracious God. There we will receive his mercy, and we will find grace to help us when we need it most.
Hebrews 4:16 NLT

May grace and peace be multiplied to you through the knowledge of God and of Jesus our Lord.
II Peter 1:2 HCSB

And the apostles were giving testimony with great power to the resurrection of the Lord Jesus, and great grace was on all of them.
Acts 4:33 HCSB

day 1

"My grace is sufficient for you,
for my power is made perfect in weakness."
Therefore I will boast all the more gladly of my weaknesses,
so that the power of Christ may rest upon me.

II Corinthians 12:9 ESV

PRAYER:

Father, I love You and trust You. I receive the covering of Your grace and the power of Christ in me today.

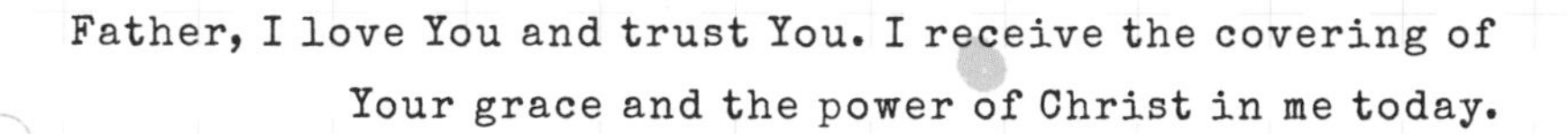

DON'T BE AFRAID

What a number of promises God makes in this verse! He will be with you, strengthen you, help you, and uphold you—all with His righteous right hand. God doesn't simply keep track of you from a distance—He knows every detail about your life, and He is with you now empowering you to overcome whatever obstacle is in your way or burden you may be carrying. That's His promise—believe it!

The LORD is the stronghold of my life—
of whom should I be afraid?
Psalm 27:1 NIV

Let the mighty strength of the Lord
make you strong.
Ephesians 6:10 CEV

You have given me your shield of victory.
Your right hand supports me;
your help has made me great.
Psalm 18:35 NLT

day 2

Do not fear, for I am with you; do not be dismayed,
for I am your God. I will strengthen you and help you;
I will uphold you with my righteous right hand.
Isaiah 41:10 NIV

Lord, I will not be afraid, because I know You—
God of creation—are with me and for me throughout this day.

NOTHING IS TOO DIFFICULT FOR GOD

Are you facing a challenge that is so big it would be easy to lose hope and give up? Rest assured that what seems like an impossible task to you is an infinitesimally small matter for God to handle. *Nothing* is too complicated or difficult for Him to work out. Rest in His care, trust in His provision, and look with anticipation at how He will come through for you—because He will.

Ah, Sovereign LORD, you have made the heavens and the earth by your great power and outstretched arm. Nothing is too hard for you.
Jeremiah 32:17 NIV

Jesus looked at [the disciples] and said, "With man it is impossible, but not with God. For all things are possible with God."
Mark 10:27 ESV

The Mighty God, the Eternal—God of past, present, and future—has spoken over the world, calling together all things from sunrise to sunset.
Psalm 50:1 VOICE

day 3

Behold, I am the LORD,
the God of all flesh;
is anything too difficult for Me?
Jeremiah 32:27 NASB

Father, I believe it when You say
that nothing is too difficult for You.
You are God over all—
so I surrender my cares to You now.

BE STILL

What? How can you be still when there are so many things grabbing for your attention?! There are always deadlines to meet and commitments to fulfill. But that's exactly why God wants you to not only be still, but also to remember that He is God. Otherwise all other things and activities might become your god without you even realizing it.

Won't you stop, meditate, and reflect on His goodness now? Doing so will bring peace to your heart as you focus on the insurmountable greatness of His love.

Now therefore stand still and see this great thing
that the LORD will do before your eyes.
I Samuel 12:16 ESV

Be exalted, LORD, in Your strength;
we will sing and praise Your might.
Psalm 21:13 HCSB

"I am God Almighty. Live in My
presence and be blameless."
Genesis 17:1 HCSB

day 4

Be still, and know that I am God.
I will be exalted among the nations,
I will be exalted in the earth!

Psalm 46:10 ESV

Lord, yes, I want to be still—I will be still—
and breathe in Your spirit.
I give You all praise now for who You are,
almighty God and Lord of my life!

YOUR DESIRES, GOD'S PURPOSE

Inhaling a deep breath after a fresh spring rain, listening to morning birds burst forth in praise, being still and relishing quiet time with God—all of these experiences bring moments of delight in the Lord. And as you spend more and more time with Him, He plants seeds of desire for His purposes for you. As you give Him your heart, He sings back to yours, calling you to fulfill the exact purpose He's created you for—and it will be a masterpiece.

For it is God who is working in you,
enabling you both to desire and to work out His good purpose.
Philippians 2:13 HCSB

"For I know the plans I have for you," declares the LORD,
"plans to prosper you and not to harm you,
plans to give you hope and a future."
Jeremiah 29:11 NIV

He who started a good work in you will carry it on
to completion until the day of Christ Jesus.
Philippians 1:6 HCSB

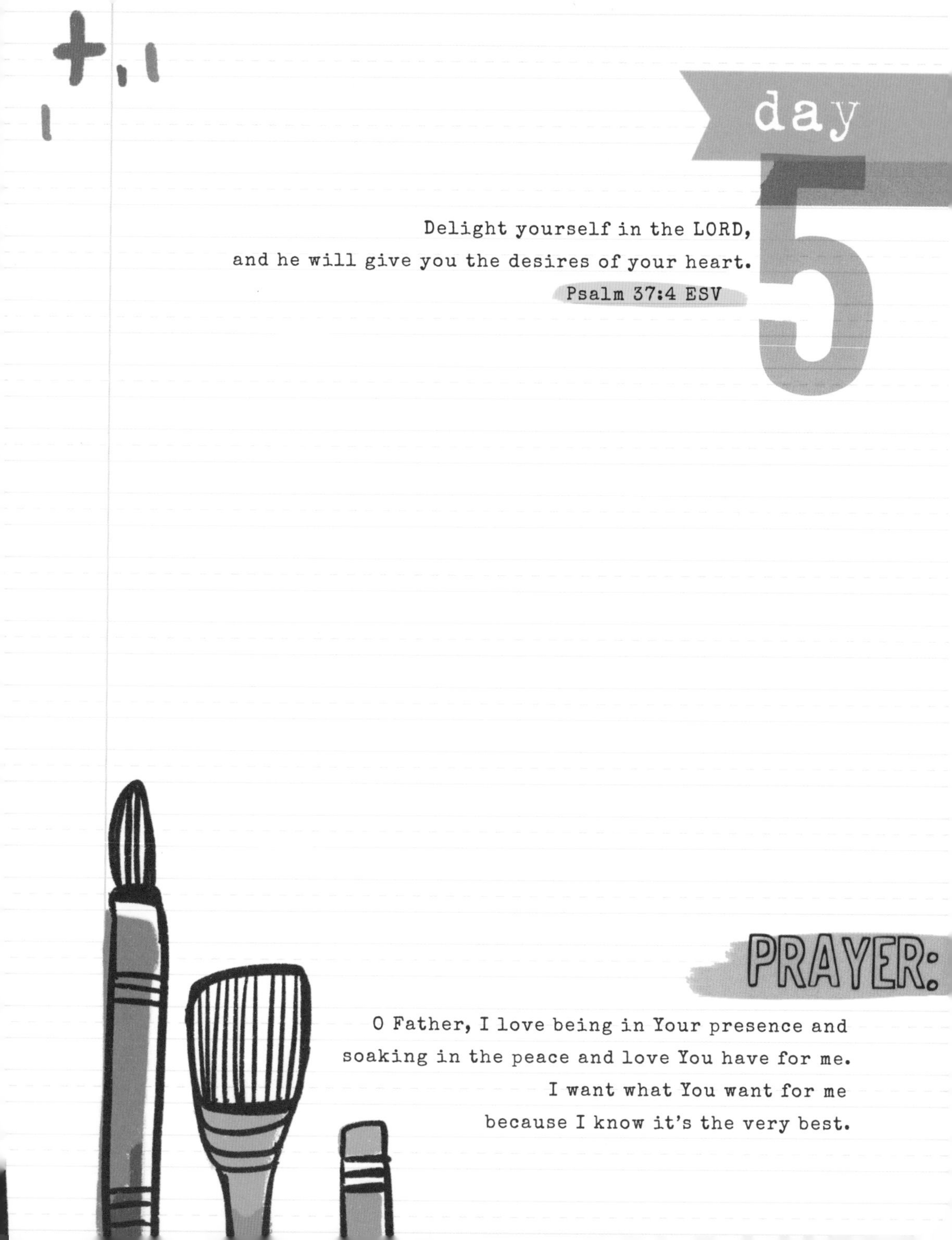

day 5

Delight yourself in the LORD,
and he will give you the desires of your heart.

Psalm 37:4 ESV

PRAYER:

O Father, I love being in Your presence and
soaking in the peace and love You have for me.
I want what You want for me
because I know it's the very best.

DON'T WORRY

It seems that when falling short or facing difficulties, the first and most natural thing to do is worry—about all the "what ifs." But what's wonderful is, Paul doesn't say "Don't worry about certain things," he says, "Don't worry about *anything.*" It's okay to bring everything that troubles you to God—nothing is too big or too insignificant. He wants you to pour out your heart and, by faith, thank Him in advance for answering and fulfilling your needs. He is waiting to hear from you.

Don't worry about your life, what you will eat
or what you will drink; or about your body,
what you will wear. Isn't life more than food
and the body more than clothing?
Matthew 6:25 HCSB

Can any of you add a cubit to his height by worrying?
Luke 12:25 HCSB

Worry weighs a person down;
an encouraging word cheers a person up.
Proverbs 12:25 NLT

day 6

Don't worry about anything, but in everything,
through prayer and petition with thanksgiving,
let your requests be made known to God.
Philippians 4:6 HCSB

PRAYER:

Lord God, help me! I don't mean to worry, but it's hard not to.
I come to You now and release the burdens from my heart to Yours.
I thank You for loving me and being a God who cares.

STEADFAST IN YOUR WORK

When working unto the Lord, no matter what that looks like, there are times when the enemy wants to make your efforts feel worthless, especially when you don't see an immediate return. But don't let that stop you from pressing forward! Even though you may not see earthly gain, you can know that as a daughter of the King, there is a far greater plan He is working out for His eternal glory. So be steadfast—He is present to help you stand firm in your faith and finish the work He's called you to do. Nothing is wasted.

Whatever you do, do it enthusiastically,
as something done for the Lord and not for men.
Colossians 3:23 HCSB

He alone shapes their hearts;
He considers all their works.
Psalm 33:15 HCSB

Faithful love belongs to You, LORD.
For You repay each according to his works.
Psalm 62:12 HCSB

INNS Consolidated, containing
Piano or Organ played from the
e Cornet played from this Edition.

day 7

Therefore, my dear [sisters], be steadfast,
immovable, always excelling in the Lord's work,
knowing that your labor in the Lord is not in vain.

I Corinthians 15:58

PRAYER:

Father, my eyes are on You and the greatness of Your power
as I do the work You've put on my heart to do.

PRAISE AT ALL TIMES

Rejoicing, praying, and expressing gratitude sound easy to do when life is going smoothly, but what about times when you're struggling just to make it through each day? Jesus knew you'd have difficult times, and His antidote for a stifled spirit is praise—not for the struggle, but to affirm His promise of eternal life with Him. He loves you. He died for you. And those are all the right reasons to rejoice in Him and be glad no matter what.

He alone is your God, the only one who is worthy of your praise,
the one who has done these mighty miracles
that you have seen with your own eyes.
Deuteronomy 10:21 NLT

Give thanks in everything,
for this is God's will for you in Christ Jesus.
I Thessalonians 5:18 HCSB

Three times a day [Daniel] got down on his knees, prayed,
and gave thanks to his God, just as he had done before.
Daniel 6:10 HCSB

day 8

Rejoice always, pray without ceasing,
give thanks in all circumstances;
for this is the will of God in Christ Jesus for you.

I Thessalonians 5:16-18 ESV

Jesus, I rejoice in You right now and
thank You from my heart for the sacrifice
You made on the cross for me.
I am truly grateful.

of God, I come! I come!
mb of God, I come! I come!
O Lamb of God, I come! I come!

NEW BEGINNINGS

Just imagine going shopping for a whole new tailored wardrobe with new shoes to match! Your old clothes would have to go to make room for all the new. That's what it's like when you accept Christ as your personal Savior—your old self is washed away and you become brand-new on the inside. Each day forward is a fresh beginning filled with God's love, hope, grace, and purpose. And the best part? New life in Christ is free!

Your old sin-loving nature was buried with him
by baptism when he died; and when God the Father,
with glorious power, brought him back to life again,
you were given his wonderful new life to enjoy.
Romans 6:4 TLB

It is God himself who has made us what we are and
given us new lives from Christ Jesus.
Ephesians 2:10 TLB

No one puts new wine into old wineskins.
Otherwise, the skins burst, the wine spills out,
and the skins are ruined. But they put new wine
into fresh wineskins, and both are preserved.
Matthew 9:17 HCSB

day 9

Anyone who belongs to Christ has become a new person.
The old life is gone; a new life has begun!

II Corinthians 5:17 NLT

Jesus, thank You for taking my old life
and replacing it with a new, Spirit-filled life of hope in You.
Don't let me look back, but rather help me
to keep looking forward and embracing the new me.

NEW MERCIES EVERY DAY

Imagine lying in bed at night, wrapped up in your sheets, and replaying the day in your mind—all the things you wished you'd done or said differently. Or maybe your soul is downcast because of an overwhelming problem. You may even wish you could hit replay and start all over. Well, you can! With each new dawn, God's love and mercies are there waiting for you to soak them in and start anew. Yesterday and its regrets are over, and His faithfulness and love are still burning strong with each new morning.

I have trusted in Your faithful love;
my heart will rejoice in Your deliverance.
Psalm 13:5 HCSB

Praise be to the God and Father of our Lord Jesus Christ.
God is the Father who is full of mercy and all comfort.
II Corinthians 1:3 NCV

Give thanks to the LORD, for He is good;
His faithful love endures forever.
I Chronicles 16:34 HCSB

day 10

The steadfast love of the LORD never ceases;
his mercies never come to an end;
they are new every morning;
great is your faithfulness.
Lamentations 3:22-23 ESV

PRAYER:

Father, I am thankful and relieved that,
because You love me so much,
Your new mercies abound in my life every day.

FREEDOM IN CONFESSION

God's Word says that sin separates us from God (Romans 6:23). But if you're not used to confessing sin, it can seem hard, especially if you're afraid of negative consequences. It's also hard because it means ridding yourself of pride so you can see what you need to confess. Yet the purpose of confession is not to tear down or condemn, it's to free you from the weight sin brings. God loves you. He is waiting on the other side of every sincere outpouring to do nothing but cleanse and renew your heart so it beats as close to His as possible.

Your iniquities have made a separation between you and your God, and your sins have hidden his face from you so that he does not hear.
Isaiah 59:2 ESV

Change your hearts and lives so you may live.
Ezekiel 18:32 ICB

Confess your sins to one another and pray for one another, so that you may be healed.
James 5:16 HCSB

day 11

If we confess our sins, he is faithful
and just to forgive us our sins and
to cleanse us from all unrighteousness.
I John 1:9 ESV

Father, I love You and want to confess my sins to You now.
Thank You for Your blessed gift of forgiveness in return.

amen

WISDOM FOR THOSE WHO ASK

Every day can bring unexpected twists and turns along with decisions to make with each one. Thank goodness there are several ways to make sure you make sound ones—by reading God's Word and through prayer. When you read your Bible and ask God for direction, He promises to provide the wisdom and guidance you need. He holds all the answers you need, and freely gives them to a heart that seeks to know His good and perfect will.

I will bless the Lord who counsels me;
he gives me wisdom in the night. He tells me what to do.
Psalm 16:7 TLB

This also comes from the LORD of hosts;
he is wonderful in counsel and excellent in wisdom.
Isaiah 28:29 ESV

Oh, the depth of the riches both of the wisdom
and the knowledge of God! How unsearchable His judgments
and untraceable His ways!
Romans 11:33 HCSB

day 12

If any of you lacks wisdom, you should ask God, who gives generously to all without finding fault, and it will be given to you.

James 1:5 NIV

PRAYER:

Lord, I need Your wisdom and direction for my life. I want to make good and healthy decisions that bring blessing and keep me in Your will for me.

COURAGE INSTEAD OF FEAR

Speaking in front of people, getting laid off from a job, staring at an empty bank account—fear can overtake your mind through all kinds of triggers. But Timothy clearly states that fear is not of God—it's the enemy's way of keeping you in a state of defeat! Thankfully, God gives power to overcome your fears. He instills power and courage into your spirit that will disable and conquer whatever ties your stomach in knots. There are no limitations. So the next time you feel afraid, claim that power and keep moving forward!

Do not fear, for I am with you; do not be afraid,
for I am your God. I will strengthen you; I will help you;
I will hold on to you with My righteous right hand.
Isaiah 41:10 HCSB

In God, whose word I praise, in God I trust;
I will not fear. What can man do to me?
Psalm 56:4 HCSB

Immediately Jesus spoke to [the disciples].
"Have courage! It is I. Don't be afraid."
Matthew 14:27 HCSB

day 13

For God has not given us a spirit of fear
and timidity, but of power, love,
and self-discipline.
II Timothy 1:7 NLT

PRAYER:

Lord, thank You for Your help, Your power,
Your strength to overcome all of the things that cause me to fear.
I am ready to live in peace and calm, no matter what I am facing.

A SPIRIT-LED LIFE

Looking to Christ and letting Him lead in all that you do yields the most beautiful testimony for drawing others to Him. Your countenance of peace and joy, your gestures of kindness and goodness, your gentle responses of self-control all run contrary to how people who don't know Christ live. So when you lead such a beautiful Spirit-led life, others see Jesus in you and, ultimately, want to know Him too. That is the highest calling anyone can have.

Let your graciousness be known to everyone.
The Lord is near.
Philippians 4:5 HCSB

A ruler can be persuaded through patience,
and a gentle tongue can break a bone.
Proverbs 25:15 HCSB

Splendor and majesty are before Him;
strength and joy are in His place.
I Chronicles 16:27 HCSB

day 14

But when the Holy Spirit controls our lives
he will produce this kind of fruit in us:
love, joy, peace, patience, kindness, goodness,
faithfulness, gentleness and self-control.

Galatians 5:22-23 TLB

Lord, I love that, through the power of Your Spirit,
I am able to experience so much change
on the inside of myself. I could not
have these qualities without You.

TAKING THOUGHTS CAPTIVE

Did you know that your mind literally expands on whatever you focus on? In other words, if you focus on what you're afraid of, your mind expands with fear and gloom. If you think about what you're grateful for, your mind expands with optimism and contentment. So if you start your day with negative thoughts, stop! Make a conscious decision to take those thoughts captive and think on whatever is true and pure and lovely. After you do, the feelings will follow and before you know it, peace will rule your day. Give it a try!

I have asked one thing from the LORD; it is what I desire:
to dwell in the house of the LORD all the days of my life,
gazing on the beauty of the LORD and seeking Him in His temple.
Psalm 27:4 HCSB

I stay awake through the night to think about your promises.
Psalm 119:148 TLB

I pray that He may grant you, according to the riches of His glory,
to be strengthened with power in the inner man through His Spirit,
and that the Messiah may dwell in your hearts through faith.
Ephesians 3:16-17 HCSB

day 15

Finally [sisters], whatever is true,
whatever is honorable, whatever is just,
whatever is pure, whatever is lovely,
whatever is commendable—if there is
any moral excellence and if there is any praise—
dwell on these things.

Philippians 4:8 HCSB

O Lord, please help me take my thoughts captive
to nothing but Your goodness and mercy in my life.
I love You and want to walk in a spirit of joy
no matter what I face today

GOD'S POWER IN YOU

Christ is in you! Yes, His Spirit resides in your heart, which means His power is yours for the taking whenever you call on His name. Whom on earth do you fear? Christ's authority is greater. What is the enemy whispering in your mind to crush your spirit? Jesus says you are able if you will trust Him. But just as a lamp cannot shine unless it's plugged in, the power of Christ won't activate without faith and belief. So call on Him today. Draw from His supernatural strength that is within you, and He will help you accomplish whatever task is before you.

For the kingdom of God is not a matter of talk but of power.
I Corinthians 4:20 HCSB

"You will not succeed by your own strength or by your own power, but by my Spirit," says the LORD All-Powerful.
Zechariah 4:6 NCV

Who is this King of glory?
The LORD, strong and mighty,
the LORD, mighty in battle.
Psalm 24:8 HCSB

day 16

Greater is He who is in you
than he who is in the world.

I John 4:4 NASB

Lord, I claim the power of Your Spirit,
which is in me to help me overcome
and be strong to face my fears!

HE SUPPLIES ALL YOUR NEEDS

It's so easy to become anxious about all the what-ifs tomorrow may, or may not, bring. But here, Jesus says exactly what to do in any given day or circumstance—seek God's kingdom first and foremost. That means putting both palms up and saying, "Okay, God, I trust You and believe that as I live out this day for Your glory and do what You lead me to do, You will provide everything You know I need." That includes peace of mind that passes all understanding to rule in your heart.

The one who lives righteously and speaks rightly,
. . . he will dwell on the heights;
his refuge will be the rocky fortresses,
his food provided, his water assured.
Isaiah 33:15-16 HCSB

He gives food to those who trust him;
he never forgets his promises.
Psalm 111:5 TLB

He who supplies seed to the sower and bread for food will supply and multiply your seed for sowing and increase the harvest of your righteousness.
II Corinthians 9:10 ESV

day 17

Seek the Kingdom of God above all else,
and live righteously, and he will
give you everything you need.

Matthew 6:33 NLT

PRAYER:

Father, I give You praise and thanksgiving
as I walk in faith believing that every need
I am tempted to worry about is already fulfilled.

WORRY . . . OR PEACE?

Have you ever stood Domino tiles in a row, then tipped the first one and watched the rest fall down consecutively? It's a good representation of the chain reaction your mind takes when you dwell on something. When you think on something bad, negative thoughts, actions, and stress will follow. But when you turn your thoughts toward God and His goodness—through prayer, Scripture, or praise—He fills you with His peace. Hmmm . . . worry and stress, or God's peace. Which will you choose today?

Trust in the LORD with all your heart,
and do not rely on your own understanding;
think about Him in all your ways,
and He will guide you on the right paths.
Proverbs 3:5–6 HCSB

You have been raised to life with Christ.
Now set your heart on what is in heaven,
where Christ rules at God's right side.
Colossians 3:1 CEV

And the effect of righteousness will be peace,
and the result of righteousness,
quietness and trust forever.
Isaiah 32:17 ESV

day 18

He will keep in perfect peace
all those who trust in him,
whose thoughts turn often to the Lord!
Isaiah 26:3 TLB

PRAYER:

Lord, I claim Your perfect peace now
as I dwell on You and all the many ways
You have been faithful and true in my life.

TRUST IN THE LORD

If there's a single word that describes life, it's *unpredictable*. One day you are motivated and ready to tackle whatever is before you, and the next you're wondering *How did I get here? This is not what I had in mind for my life!* This is why God says not to trust in yourself or your circumstances—that combination will lead to disaster. Instead, trust in Him completely. He is with you and He is for you. When you're focused on seeking and doing His will, He will light your path in the way you should go. You can trust that!

Search for the LORD and for His strength;
seek His face always.
I Chronicles 16:11 HCSB

Those who know Your name trust in You
because You have not abandoned those who seek You, Yahweh.
Psalm 9:10 HCSB

May the God of hope fill you with all joy
and peace as you trust in him,
so that you may overflow with hope
by the power of the Holy Spirit.
Romans 15:13 NIV

day 19

Trust in the LORD with all your heart;
do not depend on your own understanding.
Seek his will in all you do,
and he will show you which path to take.

Proverbs 3:5-6 NLT

PRAYER:

Father, I may not understand what's happening in Your overall plan for my life, but I know I can trust You—and that's enough for me.

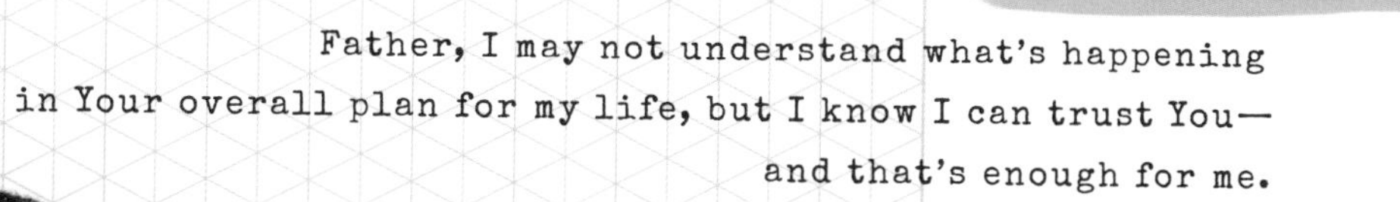

GOD'S WORD IS ALIVE

If you ever need to know how to clean, assemble, change, remove, or repair something around your house, YouTube has great videos for getting help fast. But what about when you need help with your life? There's only one reliable source for that, and it's God's Word. It's not only alive, it's been "updated" for your very situation. As you read in faith, God will literally lead you to the exact passage you need for knowing what to do in any situation. It's no less than miraculous, but then, our God is an awesome God who loves and cares for you!

But the [seed] sown on the good ground—
this is one who hears and understands the word,
who does bear fruit and yields: some 100,
some 60, some 30 times what was sown.
Matthew 13:23 HCSB

Joyful are people of integrity,
who follow the instructions of the LORD.
Psalm 119:1 NLT

I have written to you, . . . because you are strong,
God's word remains in you,
and you have had victory over the evil one.
I John 2:14 HCSB

day 20

For the word of God is living and effective and sharper than any double-edged sword, penetrating as far as the separation of soul and spirit, joints and marrow. It is able to judge the ideas and thoughts of the heart.

Hebrews 4:12 HCSB

PRAYER:

Father, I love Your beautiful Word! It is alive and active—and I feel so much closer to You when I read it. Thank You for Your guidance, instruction, and promises that are found throughout. Your Word is a gift!

ARE YOU CONTENT?

If you were to close your eyes and think about your life today, would you say that you are content with where you are and with what you have? Most people would say, "*No!* You don't know what I'm going through!" Yet Paul, shackled in chains in a prison cell, was content. No whining. No grumbling. But he wasn't able to be content by his own will—it was a state of mind he learned by drawing on God's power and strength. So, while it may not be easy, by Paul's example and with God's help, it is entirely possible to be content in your life. Yes, exactly as it is.

Godliness with contentment is great gain.
I Timothy 6:6 NIV

Keep your lives free from the love of money,
and be satisfied with what you have. God has said,
"I will never leave you; I will never abandon you."
Hebrews 13:5 NCV

For the sake of Christ, then,
I am content with weaknesses,
insults, hardships, persecutions, and calamities.
For when I am weak, then I am strong.
II Corinthians 12:10 ESV

day 21

I know what it is to be in need,
and I know what it is to have plenty.
I have learned the secret of being content in any
and every situation, whether well fed or hungry,
whether living in plenty or in want.
I can do all this through him
who gives me strength.
Philippians 4:12 NIV

PRAYER:

Lord, forgive my grumbling and lack of contentment
with what I have. You haven't failed me yet,
so I thank You now for blessing me so abundantly.

CHRIST DOESN'T CHANGE

The one thing most everyone will agree on is that change is certain—change of seasons, change of jobs, change in appearance as you grow older, change of heart as you experience both good and trying times. Some changes are for your benefit, while others test your faith. That is why it's so assuring to know One who has never changed and never will—Jesus. He is unwavering in His devotion, steadfast in His promises, and eternal in His love. He is the one and only Rock that won't be moved or manipulated. Ever. Shout all praise to Him!

For I the LORD do not change; therefore you,
O children of Jacob, are not consumed.
Malachi 3:6 ESV

Every good gift and every perfect gift is from above,
coming down from the Father of lights,
with whom there is no variation or shadow due to change.
James 1:17 ESV

Because God wanted to make the unchanging nature
of His purpose very clear to the heirs of what was promised,
He confirmed it with an oath.
Hebrews 6:17 NIV

day

22

Jesus Christ is the same yesterday,
today, and forever.

Hebrews 13:8 NLT

PRAYER:

Father, thank goodness that, while my life, the people in my life, and circumstances around me change, You remain constant and secure. In You I place my hope and trust.

WHO WILL YOU SERVE?

Every morning when you wake up, you have a very important question to answer: "Whom will I serve?" Will you hold your agenda tight with your fingers, or will you open your hands and humbly ask God what He wants you to do? It's not easy! "Self" battles for front seat, first choice, and final say. God is a second thought only when something doesn't go as planned. But this verse in Joshua is a good reminder to remember His faithfulness, get "self" off the throne, and choose to honor and serve Him.

Be sure to continue to obey all of the commandments
Moses gave you. Love the Lord and
follow his plan for your lives.
Cling to him and serve him enthusiastically.
Joshua 22:5 TLB

Serve the LORD with gladness!
Come into his presence with singing!
Psalm 100:2 ESV

And Jesus answered him,
"It is written: Worship the Lord your God,
and serve Him only."
Luke 4:8 HCSB

day 23

As for me and my house,
we will serve the LORD.
Joshua 24:15 ESV

Lord, I choose You today.
I release my plans and make myself available
and willing to serve however and wherever You lead!

PUT ON THE ARMOR OF GOD

Whether or not you want to admit it, you're in a battle. Every day that you profess your love for Jesus, the enemy gets busy trying to discourage you, overwhelm you, and get you to doubt God. That is why He gives special armor for your mind and spirit. When you are fully armed, every one of Satan's grand attempts to bring you down gets deflected into a crumb bouncing on the floor. So when you pray, put on God's armor from head to toe every day—then you can stand firm and claim *triumph* in every battle!

The one who lives under the protection
of the Most High dwells in the shadow of the Almighty.
Psalm 91:1 HCSB

The name of Yahweh is a strong tower;
the righteous run to it and are protected.
Proverbs 18:10 HCSB

Rescue me from my enemies, LORD;
I run to you to hide me.
Psalm 143:9 NLT

day 24

Put on the full armor of God so that
you can stand against the tactics of the Devil.
For our battle is not against flesh and blood,
but against . . . the spiritual forces of evil
in the heavens.

Ephesians 6:11-12 HCSB

PRAYER:

O God, I put on Your armor now!
From head to toe, cloth me with Your protection,
and keep me in the shelter of Your wings.

GOD'S LOVE IS ALWAYS THERE

Is there something you've done in your past that is so bad, you are convinced that God would never love you the way He loves other "good" people? Well, dear one, that is the enemy telling you a lie. The instant you accept Jesus as your Savior, you are forgiven, and there is nothing that can separate you from His love! *Nothing!* The depth and width of the Grand Canyon, or even the distance from earth to the heavens—nothing is too big or too bad to keep you from being His beloved child.

For as high as the heavens are above the earth,
so great is His faithful love toward those who fear Him.
Psalm 103:11 HCSB

Therefore I tell you, her many sins have been forgiven;
that's why she loved much.
Luke 7:47 HCSB

Show me the wonders of your great love,
you who save by your right hand those
who take refuge in you from their foes.
Psalm 17:7 NIV

day 25

For I am persuaded
that not even death or life,
angels or rulers, thing present or things
to come, hostile powers, height or depth,
or any other created thing will have the
power to separate us from the love of God
that is in Christ Jesus our Lord!
Romans 8:38-39 HCSB

PRAYER:

Thank You, Father, for forgiveness and for Your great love for me!

FINDING STRENGTH IN TRUST

Eagles are no less than stunning and majestic birds in God's creation. Their wingspan can get up to seven and a half feet, and they can glide at altitudes of ten thousand feet for hours. They do this by finding wind thermals that literally carry them for miles so they're able to save energy and soar for very long distances. Likewise, when you trust in the Lord, your spirit gets swept up in His spiritual thermal that carries you above any mountain you're climbing or through whatever valley you're crawling in. So abide in His trust and rest in His strength. You will see a breathtaking view of just how magnificent and swift His love is for you.

My grace is sufficient for you,
for my power is made perfect in weakness.
II Corinthians 12:9 ESV

He gives power to the tired and worn out,
and strength to the weak.
Isaiah 40:29 TLB

The LORD is my strength and my shield; my heart trusts in
Him, and I am helped. Therefore my heart rejoices,
and I praise Him with my song.
Psalm 28:7 HCSB

day 26

Those who trust in the LORD
will find new strength. They will soar high
on wings like eagles. They will run and
not grow weary. They will walk and not faint.

Isaiah 40:31 NLT

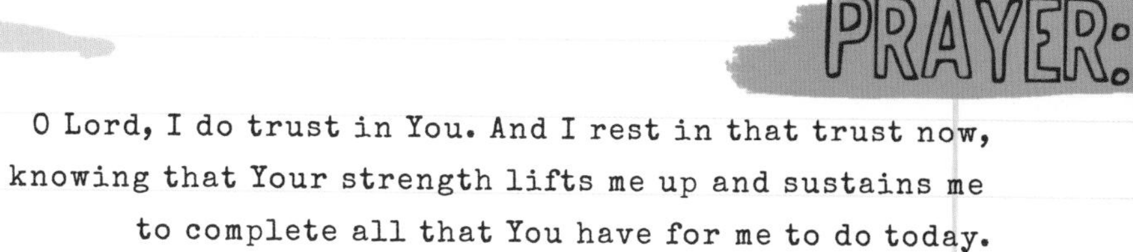

PRAYER:

O Lord, I do trust in You. And I rest in that trust now,
knowing that Your strength lifts me up and sustains me
to complete all that You have for me to do today.

LIVE WITH ENDURANCE

When long-distance runners race, they settle into a pace that enables them to run for miles without tiring. This pace doesn't come naturally but rather by spending months, even years, training and focusing on their goal so this "sweet spot" becomes second nature. You also have a sweet spot in your race of life that enables you to fulfill God's call for you. By daily fixing your eyes, your mind, your heart, and your activities on Jesus, He leads and empowers you to run with endurance until you celebrate your finish line in victory!

For whatever was written in the past
was written for our instruction,
so that we may have hope through endurance
and through the encouragement from the Scriptures.
Romans 15:4 HCSB

Give careful thought to the paths
for your feet and be steadfast in all your ways.
Proverbs 4:26 NIV

I will meditate on your precepts and fix my eyes on your ways.
Psalm 119:15 ESV

day 27

Let us run with endurance the race that lies before us, keeping our eyes on Jesus, the source and perfecter of our faith.

Hebrews 12:1-2 HCSB

Lord, I look to You now. Please, place blinders on each side of my face so that all I see is You throughout this day and keep growing stronger in my faith.

GOD'S GOODNESS IN ALL THINGS

Have you ever put together a jigsaw puzzle with hundreds of tiny pieces and a detailed picture to recreate? The process can be slow and tedious, and the picture remains incomplete for a long time. The same can be said for your life. Some days or pieces are strenuous, jagged, or ugly; some don't even make sense for what God has called you to do. But He sees the bigger, final picture He created you for. So whatever piece you are living today, know that it has a purpose—God fits each day and experience together to create a beautiful masterpiece in the end.

I call to God Most High,
to God who fulfills His purpose for me.
Psalm 57:2 HCSB

All the paths of the LORD are lovingkindness
and truth to those who keep His covenant and His testimonies.
Psalm 25:10 NASB

Trust in the LORD with all your heart,
and do not rely on your own understanding;
think about Him in all your ways,
and He will guide you on the right paths.
Proverbs 3:5-6 HCSB

day 28

And we know that all things work together for good to them that love God, to them who are the called according to his purpose.

Romans 8:28 KJV

Father, even though I don't understand some things in my life, I know You are in control, and I will trust in Your ways.

BE STRONG!

In this verse, God is not suggesting that Joshua be strong and courageous, He's *commanding* it! Now, you could take this command and make it very personal by inserting your name. Go on, give it a try . . . "Haven't I commanded you, _______________: be strong and courageous?" Dear one, whatever has you in a state of weakness, discouragement, or fear, you have God's promise that He is with you. That means not only do you have His strength and courage to draw from, He commands you to take it. Will you?

Do not fear, for I am with you;
do not be afraid, for I am your God.
I will strengthen you; I will help you;
I will hold on to you with My righteous right hand.
Isaiah 41:10 HCSB

Immediately Jesus spoke to them.
"Have courage! It is I. Don't be afraid."
Matthew 14:27 HCSB

In God, whose word I praise, in God I trust;
I will not fear. What can man do to me?
Psalm 56:4 HCSB

day 29

Haven't I commanded you:
be strong and courageous?
Do not be afraid or discouraged,
for the LORD your God is with you
wherever you go.
Joshua 1:9 HCSB

Okay, Lord, I will be strong and courageous.
I receive Your power now to face my fears and, one day at a time,
overcome them once and for all.

CONFESS AND BE HEALED

Holding onto sin is much like a dam that holds back water: until the sin is confessed and healing has replaced the damage that sin caused, the capacity of your prayers is held back. But when you ask someone you've hurt for forgiveness or acknowledge a lie or a grumbling attitude, healing and renewal take place, and the floodgates of righteousness are opened! At that very moment, God rushes straight to your heart and instills peace that passes understanding and a newfound boldness to approach His throne in prayer.

When I kept silent, my bones became brittle . . .
my strength was drained as in the summer's heat.
Then I acknowledged my sin to You . . . I said,
"I will confess my transgressions to the LORD,"
and You took away the guilt of my sin.
Psalm 32:3–5 HCSB

The one who conceals his sins will not prosper,
but whoever confesses and renounces them will find mercy.
Proverbs 28:13 HCSB

Go and learn what this means: I desire mercy and not sacrifice.
For I didn't come to call the righteous, but sinners.
Matthew 9:13 HCSB

day 30

So own up to your sins to one another
and pray for one another. In the end,
you may be healed. Your prayers are powerful
when they are rooted in a righteous life.

James 5:16 VOICE

Lord, I confess to You now all that I know displeases You—
all that runs contrary to Your Word.
I am so very grateful for Your forgiveness and
for renewing my strength with a readiness to do Your will.

GOD IS ALWAYS NEAR ME.
(Elementary.) Eleanor Smith.

GOD'S PLANS FOR YOU

When you think of your future, what comes to mind? Visions of what you hope will be? Dreams of experiences you wish for? The fact is, you simply can't foretell exactly what will happen, but God can. He not only knows your future, He's planned it! And the beautiful promise within those plans is, they are good and full of hope. What a pleasing and comforting thought to hold on to!

I call to God Most High,
to God who fulfills His purpose for me.
Psalm 57:2 HCSB

Let the Lord Jesus Christ be as near to you
as the clothes you wear. Then you won't try
to satisfy your selfish desires.
Romans 13:14 CEV

How happy is everyone who fears the LORD,
who walks in His ways!
Psalm 128:1 HCSB

day 31

"I know what I am planning for you,"
says the LORD. "I have good plans for you,
not plans to hurt you.
I will give you hope and a good future."
Jeremiah 29:11 NCV

Lord, I know You are a good God and that You love me.
So I trust in You as I commit to Your plans
and live out Your purposes for me.

LIVING GOD'S WAY IN THIS WORLD

One of the biggest challenges with living in this world is doing so without conforming to it. That means living your life God's way instead of what's popular or expected by people who don't share your love for God. But this is hard without spending time reading and meditating on His Word. The world's way is often innocent looking and even beautiful on the surface. But when you know what God says about a given situation and you are led by His Spirit, you're able to discern His will and be a shining light for Him—which is always good, pleasing, and perfect.

You took off your former way of life, the old self . . .
put on the new self, the one created according to God's likeness
in righteousness and purity of the truth.
Ephesians 4:22–24 HCSB

Joyful are people of integrity,
who follow the instructions of the LORD.
Psalm 119:1 NLT

All the LORD's ways show faithful love and truth
to those who keep His covenant and decrees.
Psalm 25:10 HCSB

day 32

Do not conform any longer to the pattern
of this world, but be transformed by
the renewing of your mind. Then you will
be able to test and approve what God's will is—
His good, pleasing and perfect will.

Romans 12:2 NIV

PRAYER:

Lord, each day is a struggle not to follow the pattern of this world.
Please help me and convict me when I start to stray. I want
to stay close to You and Your ways only.

DO NOT BE SILENT

Have you ever been afraid to share about Jesus with someone of another faith? That's exactly what Paul was doing in Corinth when the Lord spoke to him in a vision. Paul had been testifying to the Jews that Jesus was the Messiah, and they not only disagreed, they became violent and tried to have him arrested! But the Lord gave Paul reassurance that He wanted him to keep proclaiming the Good News with boldness. God doesn't expect you to do His will on your own—He is right there to help. Praise God that the same Jesus who helped Paul gives the same reassurance to you today!

For I am not ashamed of the gospel,
because it is the power of God that brings salvation
to everyone who believes.
Romans 1:16 NIV

If they do not welcome you, when you leave that town,
shake off the dust from your feet as a testimony against them.
Luke 9:5 HCSB

Therefore, my tongue will proclaim Your righteousness
all day long, for those who seek my harm will be
disgraced and confounded.
Psalm 71:24 HCSB

One night the Lord spoke to Paul in a vision: "Do not be afraid; keep on speaking, do not be silent. For I am with you, and no one is going to attack and harm you."

Acts 18:9 NIV

O God, I confess I have been afraid to speak boldly about You. Rejection is hard to receive. But by Paul's example and the strength You provide, I will share of Your goodness and love.

CHRIST DIED FOR YOU

When you look at and think on the word *sinner*, there is no good or just thought to put with it—sin is all that is bad. And yet, while all of humanity was full of sin, God in all His humility, goodness, and love poured down His holy oil of grace—Jesus—to remove sin's effects on all who receive Him. That is pure love.

"It is an unseemly sight to see God humbling Himself and man exalting himself; to see a humble Savior and a proud sinner."

—THOMAS WATSON

For I passed on to you as most important what I also received:
that Christ died for our sins according to the Scriptures.
I Corinthians 15:3 HCSB

For while we were still helpless,
at the right time
Christ died for the ungodly.
Romans 5:6 NASB

He humbled Himself by becoming obedient to the point of death—
even to death on a cross.
Philippians 2:8 HCSB

day 34

But God demonstrates his own love for us in this:
While we were still sinners, Christ died for us.

Romans 5:8 NIV

Lord, thank You for dying for me.
My gratitude runs to the core of my heart. I love You.

4. He with earth - ly cares en - twin - eth Hope and com - fort from a - bove:

CHRIST IS IN YOU

As soon as you accept Christ as your personal Savior, His Spirit takes up residence in your heart! He lives there to love, to forgive, and to intercede on your behalf when you pray to God the Father. Your physical body is still alive, but the Spirit of Jesus is in authority to lead and guide you, to speak to you, to give supernatural strength and courage and whatever else you need to live out God's call on your life. By faith and belief in God's Son, you are no longer living on your own—He is in you!

But when the Father sends the Comforter instead of me—
and by the Comforter I mean the Holy Spirit—
he will teach you much, as well as remind you
of everything I myself have told you.
John 14:26 TLB

For to me to live is Christ,
and to die is gain.
Philippians 1:21 ESV

But God proves His own love for us
in that while we were still sinners, Christ died for us!
Romans 5:8 HCSB

day 35

I no longer live, but Christ lives in me.
The life I now live in the body,
I live by faith in the Son of God,
who loved me and gave Himself for me.

Galatians 2:20 HCSB

PRAYER:

Lord, please, may Your spirit lead me and guide me today!
Keep me within the bounds of Your calling on my life,
and watch over me as I step out in faith.

WAIT ON HIS TIMING

Is there something you are waiting on God for today? Maybe a decision you need help with, or whether or not you got the new job, or for His mighty intervention in a loved one's life. It takes a lot of strength and courage of heart not to take matters into your own hands, doesn't it? Yet that is exactly what He wants you to do—wait on His perfect timing for the unfolding of His perfect plan. He is with you and in absolute control, so trust in Him as you wait.

I wait for Yahweh;
I wait and put my hope in His word.
Psalm 130:5 HCSB

Therefore the LORD is waiting to show you mercy,
and is rising up to show you compassion,
for the LORD is a just God.
All who wait patiently for Him are happy.
Isaiah 30:18 HCSB

Let your hope make you glad.
Be patient in time of trouble
and never stop praying.
Romans 12:12 CEV

day

36

Wait for the LORD; be strong,
and let your heart take courage;
wait for the LORD!
Psalm 27:14 ESV

PRAYER:

O Lord, waiting with patience is hard.
But I trust in You and know that Your timing
is absolutely perfect in all things. So I will wait.

can see me just as well As by morn - ing light.
a look or word or thought, But God knows it all. A - men.

JOY IN TROUBLES

Wait . . . great *joy* in troubles?! This seems to be a mistake, yet that's what the verse says. But when you think about it, there must be resistance applied for muscles to grow strong. And the more intense the resistance, the more pressure one is able to endure for longer periods of time. So the next time a trial comes into your life, rejoice in knowing your spiritual stamina is being developed so that, instead of getting knocked to pieces, you'll remain steadfast in hope and sweetened with God's peace. What a great testimony to others who don't know Christ!

We also rejoice in our afflictions,
because we know that affliction produces endurance,
endurance produces proven character,
and proven character produces hope.
Romans 5:3-4 HCSB

For you have need of endurance, so that when you have done
the will of God you may receive what is promised.
Hebrews 10:36 ESV

I will rejoice and be glad in Your faithful love
because You have seen my affliction.
You have known the troubles of my life.
Psalm 31:7 HCSB

day

37

When troubles of any kind come your way,
consider it an opportunity for great joy.
For you know that when your faith is tested,
your endurance has a chance to grow.

James 1:2-3 NLT

PRAYER:

Lord, I understand the purpose of building endurance—life is hard! Please help me with the joy part. This is where I struggle. To have joy in a trial is something I want, so I will start now by giving thanks for Your faithfulness.

AUTHENTIC FAITH

Isn't it wonderful how God doesn't require you to have a large amount of faith in order to act in your life? He understands the struggle to believe in something you can't see, so He doesn't expect faith the size of Mt. Rushmore! No, you only need to have a small amount, just so long as it's real. Authentic faith the size of a dot can move a mountain. So, what is He convicting you to have faith in Him for? Believe . . . trust . . . have genuine faith that He will do what He says He will do.

But I have trusted in Your faithful love;
my heart will rejoice in Your deliverance.
Psalm 13:5 HCSB

But He said to them, "Why are you fearful,
you of little faith?"
Then He got up and rebuked the winds and the sea.
And there was a great calm.
Matthew 8:26 HCSB

"Go your way," Jesus told him.
"Your faith has healed you."
Immediately he could see and
began to follow Him on the road.
Mark 10:52 HCSB

day 38

For I assure you: If you have faith the size of a mustard seed, you will tell this mountain, "Move from here to there" and it will move. Nothing will be impossible for you.

Matthew 17:20 HCSB

Yes, Lord, I trust You and have faith that You are true to Your promises. You have never failed me in the past, so I have faith that You are with me now and in my future.

DRAWING OTHERS TO JESUS

Your life is a living testimony to everyone you encounter. People are watching you remain calm while others come unglued. They're noticing the peace you have when circumstances are chaotic. They want to know why you'd forgive someone when they would lash back. Sooner or later, people will notice you are different—that you have something they don't—and they'll want it for themselves. That's why it's so important not only to be ready to share your faith but to speak in love. People are drawn to Jesus by the love He has for them through you!

Then the woman left her water jar, went into town,
and told the men, "Come, see a man who told me
everything I ever did! Could this be the Messiah?"
They left the town and made their way to Him.
John 4:28-30 HCSB

But when they believed Philip,
as he preached the good news about the kingdom of God
and the name of Jesus Christ,
both men and women were baptized.
Acts 8:12 HCSB

And they departed and went through the villages,
preaching the gospel and healing everywhere.
Luke 9:6 ESV

day 39

Always be prepared to give an answer
to everyone who asks you to give the reason
for the hope that you have.
But do this with gentleness and respect.
I Peter 3:15 NIV

O Lord, help me to always be ready to share about You
and Your saving grace and faithfulness to all.

THE LOVE OF MONEY

Money: it takes a lot of it to buy all the things you need and want! There's nothing wrong with having lots of money . . . as long as you don't fall in love with it. People who love money become so focused on "things," the weeds of greed take root and push out God and people. But our God is a jealous God—He wants to be the utmost focus of your mind and heart. He wants you to know that if you have a lot of money or only a little, He is the only Source of true and lasting contentment. And that is something money cannot buy.

But those who want to be rich fall into temptation, a trap,
and many foolish and harmful desires,
which plunge people into ruin and destruction.
I Timothy 6:9 HCSB

I know what it is to be in need,
and I know what it is to have plenty.
I have learned the secret of being content
in any and every situation.
Philippians 4:12 NIV

And my God will supply all your needs
according to His riches
in glory in Christ Jesus.
Philippians 4:19 HCSB

day 40

Keep your lives free from the love
of money and be content with what you have,
because God has said, "Never will I leave you;
never will I forsake you."

Hebrews 13:5 NIV

PRAYER:

Father, You have been ever so faithful to fulfill my needs.
Help me to be content by being grateful for what I have
and truly receiving the fullness of Your grace.

YOU ARE GOD'S WORKMANSHIP

What a compliment Paul gives here to your value in God! To be God's workmanship means that He took qualities of His own and imparted them—through Christ—into you! Does that give you chills?! He did this because He has work for you to do—His work. He has prepared you, equipped you, and gifted you to accomplish His will for your life and for His kingdom. What an honor to wear a badge of holiness and be used for His glory. Praise Jesus!

For just as the body without the spirit is dead,
so also faith is dead.
James 2:26 HCSB

All Scripture is breathed out by God and profitable . . .
for training in righteousness,
that the man of God may be complete,
equipped for every good work.
II Timothy 3:16-17 ESV

You, however, are not in the flesh, but in the Spirit,
since the Spirit of God lives in you.
Romans 8:9 HCSB

day 41

For we are God's workmanship,
created in Christ Jesus to do good works,
which God prepared in advance for us to do.
Ephesians 2:10 NIV

PRAYER:

Lord God, I want to complete the work You would have me do! By Your Spirit within me, show me, lead me to the place, the time, and the people You would have me serve.

FACING TEMPTATION

Temptation is a 24/7 enticement—if one thing doesn't get you to sin, something else will come right along to catch you off guard and do the job! Fortunately, there is help for avoiding, even deflecting, temptation. First, knowing God's Word provides clear discernment for giving a right response to a wrong opportunity. Second, don't walk, run to the nearest exit. Finally, pray to Jesus and call on the power of His Spirit in you. He fights for you at every beck and call. God is bigger than your battles—He will help!

Stay awake and pray,
so that you won't enter into temptation.
The spirit is willing, but the flesh is weak.
Matthew 26:41 HCSB

And do not bring us into temptation,
but deliver us from the evil one.
[For Yours is the kingdom
and the power and the glory forever. Amen.]
Matthew 6:13 HCSB

Put on the full armor of God so that you can
stand against the tactics of the Devil.
Ephesians 6:11 HCSB

day 42

The temptations in your life are no different from what others experience. And God is faithful. He will not allow the temptation to be more than you can stand. When you are tempted, he will show you a way out so that you can endure.

I Corinthians 10:13 NLT

Lord, I call on You today to help me.
Guard me against those things that tempt me.
I want to remain faithful to You and not get distracted by anything that could hurt me or my testimony.

THE GIFT OF ETERNAL LIFE

Of all the heartwarming and hope-filled promises given in the Bible, this one is the most reassuring and life giving. When you believe that Jesus is God's Son and ask Him into your heart, you have an eternal residence with Him. It's a place reserved just for you and all other believers. Rejoice and be glad that life doesn't end here on earth—it begins and is fulfilled in the hope of eternity with the Creator of the universe!

You reveal the path of life to me;
in Your presence is abundant joy;
in Your right hand are eternal pleasures.
Psalm 16:11 HCSB

For God loved the world in this way:
He gave His One and Only Son,
so that everyone who believes in Him
will not perish but have eternal life.
John 3:16 HCSB

I give them eternal life, and they will never perish—ever!
No one will snatch them out of My hand.
John 10:28 HCSB

day 43

This is the testimony: God has given us eternal life, and this life is in His Son.

I John 5:11 HCSB

PRAYER:

Father, thank You for Your gift of eternal life with You. Thank You for the sacrifice Your Son made for me and for His Holy Spirit that is within me now. I am so very grateful.

CAST AWAY YOUR CARES

Anxiety is so debilitating. Body, mind, and spirit can plummet when filled with it, and no one is immune to its effects. But God, in His love and care for you, will take your anxiety onto Himself—just simply cast it to Him. Hurling or throwing something takes focus and force so the object being thrown lands far away from your presence. When you cast your anxiety on God, it gets caught up in His mercy net where He receives the weight anxiety brings and replaces it with His comfort and calm. Nothing is too small or too big—just cast.

And do not seek what you are to eat
and what you are to drink, nor be worried.
Luke 12:29 ESV

Don't worry about anything, but in everything,
through prayer and petition with thanksgiving,
let your requests be made known to God.
Philippians 4:6 HCSB

When you are brought into the synagogues before the leaders
and other powerful people, don't worry about
how to defend yourself or what to say.
Luke 12:11 NCV

44

Cast all your anxiety on Him
because He cares for you.
I Peter 5:7 NIV

Lord, it is so hard not to worry, but I know I shouldn't. You have taken care of me in the past, so I know You will today and in the future. I cast my cares to You now and trust that You are with me and You will provide.

JESUS HAS OVERCOME

In this verse, when Jesus said "these things" to the apostles, He was foretelling His death and resurrection, and providing assurance for them not to be afraid or worried—He would still be with them (through His Holy Spirit). His death on the cross meant taking on the sin of the world! He overcame Satan's curse of death on our behalf. Because of this, we are righteous in God's eyes and have the gift of eternal life with Him. This promise is as true today as it was then, and that is something for which to give all praise and glory. *Jesus has overcome!*

Now may the God of hope fill you with all joy and peace as you believe in Him so that you may overflow with hope by the power of the Holy Spirit.
Romans 15:13 HCSB

Then, because you belong to Christ Jesus, God will bless you with peace that no one can completely understand. And this peace will control the way you think and feel.
Philippians 4:7 CEV

Grace, mercy, and peace will be with us from God the Father and from Jesus Christ, the Son of the Father, in truth and love.
II John 1:3 HCSB

day 45

I have told you these things,
so that in me you may have peace.
In this world you will have trouble.
But take heart! I have overcome the world.
John 16:33 NIV

PRAYER:

Lord, thank You for the ultimate sacrifice
You made so that I can have eternal life with You.
I claim Your deep and calming peace now
to reside within my heart today.

GOD WILL GUIDE YOU

Seasons of life can sometimes lead to an enormously desolate place. Your compass can break and your hope can get sapped down to its last drop. But when you call upon the Lord and ask for His help, He hears. He promises to lead and guide you in the way you should go. Even better, He will give nourishment and strength for your body, and peace to satisfy your dry, parched soul. So, call on Him, look to Him—He is able and willing to bring you out of any barren wilderness. Keep your eyes on Him and believe in His goodness for you.

Yes, you are my Rock and my fortress;
honor your name by leading me out of this peril.
Psalm 31:3 TLB

You rejoice in this, though now for a short time
you have had to struggle in various trials so
that the genuineness of your faith—more valuable than gold,
which perishes though refined by fire—may result in praise,
glory, and honor at the revelation of Jesus Christ.
I Peter 1:6-7 HCSB

Even though I walk through the valley of the shadow of death,
I will fear no evil, for you are with me;
your rod and your staff, they comfort me.
Psalm 23:4 ESV

day 46

The LORD will guide you always;
he will satisfy your needs in a sun-scorched
land and will strengthen your frame.
You will be like a well-watered garden,
like a spring whose waters never fail.
Isaiah 58:11 NIV

PRAYER:

Father, I call on You now for Your presence and comfort today. Fill me with Your peace and guide my steps in the way I should go.

ENDURING THROUGH TRIALS

Being tempted or tested to do the right thing day after day when all you want to do is give up is never easy, especially when the test lasts for a lifetime. But that's how long the testing of your faith lasts! Yet when you cling to the persevering grace of God and continue to rest in the hope of salvation in Christ, a glorious crown awaits on your day of completion. Until then, you have the presence and power of God to help you and to hold onto.

No temptation has overtaken you except what is common to humanity. God is faithful, and He will not allow you to be tempted beyond what you are able, but with the temptation He will also provide a way of escape so that you are able to bear it.
I Corinthians 10:13 HCSB

Don't blame God when you are tempted! God cannot be tempted by evil, and he doesn't use evil to tempt others.
We are tempted by our own desires that drag us off and trap us.
James 1:13-14 CEV

Stay awake and pray so that you won't enter into temptation.
Mark 14:38 HCSB

day 47

A man who endures trials is blessed,
because when he passes the test
he will receive the crown of life
that God has promised to those who love Him.

James 1:12 HCSB

Father, there are so many temptations that flash before me every single day. So, one day at a time, I cling to You and the power of Your Spirit within me to walk away and help stay the course You have for me.

GOD IS WATCHING YOU

Did you by chance get up this morning and think, *God is watching me today. As much as He's got to do in the world, He is watching me!* Not from the point of trying to catch you doing something wrong, but because He adores you; watching you is His priority because He loves you. He is not distant or preoccupied with His endless To Do lists. He knows your life, your heart, and all that you need, and He's working now to provide for you to the fullest. How wonderful to know you are not alone, ever. Will you make time to look back at Him?

Then I lay down and slept in peace and woke up safely,
for the Lord was watching over me.
Psalm 3:5 TLB

Do not fear, for I am with you; do not be afraid, for I am your God.
I will strengthen you; I will help you;
I will hold on to you with My righteous right hand.
Isaiah 41:10 HCSB

Not even death or life, angels or rulers, things present or things to come, . . . or any other created thing will have the power to separate us from the love of God that is in Christ Jesus our Lord!
Romans 8:38-39 HCSB

day 48

Behold, the eye of the LORD is on those who fear him, on those who hope in his steadfast love.

Psalm 33:18 ESV

Lord, I feel so special and loved knowing You are watching me as well as watching over me.

ANGELS WATCHING OVER YOU

Wow, wherever you go, God's angels are protecting you. This raises the thought, *If angels are protecting me, it's because there is an enemy who is after me wherever I go.* Yes, and if you've just had an uneventful day, it's probably because God's army of angels has been working very hard to block the enemy's attempts to mess you up! Likewise, getting stuck behind that slow driver yesterday, or not being able to meet up with friends as planned, or any other "frustration" you've encountered could all be part of God's angels protecting you from an even greater unwanted incident. Hmmm . . . that is something to think about!

See that you don't look down on one of these little ones,
because I tell you that in heaven their angels
continually view the face of My Father in heaven.
Matthew 18:10 HCSB

My God sent His angel and shut the lions' mouths.
They haven't hurt me,
for I was found innocent before Him.
Daniel 6:22 HCSB

If you honor the LORD,
his angel will protect you.
Psalm 34:7 CEV

day 49

For he orders his angels
to protect you wherever you go.
Psalm 91:11 TLB

Lord, I get so busy each day, I forget that I have an angel protecting me. The next time things don't go as planned or I experience a near miss while driving, I'll thank You and praise You for Your protection.

DO NOT STOP MEETING TOGETHER

You know what happens when people get together on a regular basis and do church? They get to know each other! Sooner or later they start sharing what is on their hearts, they begin praying for one another, and bonds of friendship are made and strengthened. When your soul strings are tied with other Jesus lovers and prayer warriors, your body, mind, and spirit develop an impenetrable shield that keeps hope alive and tells Satan to take a dive. Making church a priority is, well, a priority. So keep going!

One day there were about one hundred twenty
of the Lord's followers meeting together,
and Peter stood up to speak to them.
Acts 1:15 CEV

And they devoted themselves to the apostles' teaching,
to the fellowship, to the breaking of bread, and to the prayers.
Acts 2:42 HCSB

If we are living in the light of God's presence,
just as Christ does, then we have wonderful fellowship
and joy with each other.
I John 1:7 TLB

day 50

And let us be concerned about one another
in order to promote love and good works,
not staying away from our worship meetings,
as some habitually do, but encouraging each other,
and all the more as you see the day drawing near.
Hebrews 10:24-25 HCSB

PRAYER:

Lord, I know that the enemy loves to keep me too busy—and tired—
to make it to church or attend small group every week.
Help me to make fellowship a priority no matter what,
because I can handle life better with support from others
than I can on my own.

QUIETNESS AND TRUST

Doesn't living in a noisy, chaotic, fast-paced world that places constant demands on your time, energy, and emotions make you want to run toward a place of quietness and trust?! When you stay focused on and committed to pleasing God, that's exactly what you'll have—His blessed assurance that all will be well with your soul. The way a laser beam locks in on a target, God streams His gift of peace and quiet and rest into your soul and guards it so no amount of disturbance can penetrate. That means for today, tomorrow, and the next—forever is this promise to you.

The LORD gives his people strength.
The LORD blesses them with peace.
Psalm 29:11 NLT

You will keep in perfect peace all who trust in you,
all whose thoughts are fixed on you!
Isaiah 26:3 NLT

Come to Me, all of you who are weary and burdened,
and I will give you rest.
Matthew 11:28 HCSB

And the effect of righteousness will be peace,
and the result of righteousness,
quietness and trust forever.

Isaiah 32:17 ESV

Father, thank You for Your peace and quiet in my soul to draw from at any time. You alone are my refuge in this crazy, busy, loud world.

WHAT'S IN THE SOIL OF YOUR HEART?

Do you remember those ads showing a plant without Miracle-Gro looking dull, sparse, and bent over, then another plant with Miracle-Gro showing huge, vibrant flowers and bushy foliage? Well, the condition of your heart is much like the soil from which the fruit of your life grows. And your spiritual Miracle-Gro yields the greatest fruit for God's kingdom imaginable. How do you get it? Through daily prayer and devotions, reading God's Word, and doing the work He's given you to do. When the soil of your heart is conditioned for God, He can and will do great and mighty things in you and for you.

Be doers of the word and not hearers only.
James 1:22 HCSB

I have treasured Your word in my heart
so that I may not sin against You.
Psalm 119:11 HCSB

So Jesus said to the Jews who had believed Him,
"If you continue in My word,
you really are My disciples."
John 8:31 HCSB

day 52

But the [seed] sown on the good ground—this is one who hears and understands the word, who does bear fruit and yields: some 100, some 60, some 30 times what was sown.

Matthew 13:23 HCSB

PRAYER:

Lord, I am so grateful for the blessings I experience through Your Word. Whenever I search the Scriptures for help, I find it. When I need comfort, Your words provide it. I love to meet You in the pages and have fellowship I never imagined possible.

JESUS UNDERSTANDS

When you feel overwhelmed or are struggling about something and you just need to vent or get help, you are most likely to call someone who's "been there," right? That person will have the empathy and compassion you need for lifting your heart out of a pit of discouragement. Problem is, your friend might not be available—she may be too busy to take a call, which is even more frustrating. But Jesus is already on the line waiting for you. And He's been through battles and temptations that brought on the very feelings you struggle with today. He's "been there" and He "is there." So next time, who're you gonna call? Christ Jesus!

Then Jesus was led out into the wilderness by the Holy Spirit,
to be tempted there by Satan.
Matthew 4:1 TLB

When He saw the crowds, He felt compassion for them,
because they were weary and worn out,
like sheep without a shepherd.
Matthew 9:36 HCSB

Going a little farther, He fell facedown and prayed,
"My Father! If it is possible,
let this cup pass from Me.
Yet not as I will, but as You will."
Matthew 26:39 HCSB

For we do not have a high priest who is unable
to sympathize with our weaknesses,
but One who has been tested in every way
as we are, yet without sin.

Hebrews 4:15 HCSB

PRAYER:

Jesus, I am so thankful that I can come to You with
my struggles and know that You completely
understand and You care. Thank You for being
my Savior and my Friend.

GOD DRAWS NEAR TO YOU

God—the all-powerful, all-knowing, almighty One who created the universe, the stars and planets, and all who have existed since the beginning of time—is a personal God. He created you because He loves you and wants fellowship with . . . you. All you have to do is draw near to Him and, no, He doesn't stand back and wait for you to reach Him. When He sees you drawing near, He approaches you in unison. He moves toward you to embrace you with His big and welcoming arms. All you have to do is still your heart and make your move. He is waiting . . .

A man of many companions may come to ruin,
but there is a friend who sticks closer than a brother.
Proverbs 18:24 ESV

Seeing their faith He said,
"Friend, your sins are forgiven you."
Luke 5:20 HCSB

You are My friends if you do what I command you.
John 15:14 HCSB

day 54

Draw near to God,
and He will draw near to you.
James 4:8 HCSB

Lord, I think of that song "What a Friend We Have in Jesus" and feel warm in knowing that You are so very close to me as a friend. I love You and want nothing more right now than to be still in Your arms.

YOUR LIFELINE OF HOPE

To believe, or not to believe: that is the question. To believe what, you wonder? Simply put, that Christ's death and resurrection was for you. And, because of that, you really and truly have direct access to God the Father now and for eternity. Holding onto this promise is your lifeline of hope when difficult circumstances on this earth come crashing down and your faith is stretched. But when you hold on, God is faithful to fill you with all assurance that He indeed is with you and reigns in your heart.

You will be confident,
because there is hope.
You will look carefully about
and lie down in safety.
Job 11:18 HCSB

But you must return to your God.
Maintain love and justice,
and always put your hope in God.
Hosea 12:6 HCSB

Because of the LORD's faithful love
we do not perish,
for His mercies never end.
Lamentations 3:22 HCSB

day 55

Let us hold on to the confession
of our hope without wavering,
for He who promised is faithful.
Hebrews 10:23 HCSB

Lord, I believe! I am so grateful for the hope I have in You.
Help me to hold onto it no matter what I face
today, tomorrow, or the next day.

CHEERFUL GIVING

When children are put together to play, it doesn't take long for one child to take another kid's toy, then—*temper tantrum!* Now imagine children playing together and one little girl picks up her toy and hands it to another girl to play with. Doesn't it make you want to give the girl praise and more toys to play with, because you know she'll see who's lacking and share what she has with them? Such is God's view of us handling the gifts He blesses us with. He loves a happy giver and provides an endless supply when we share with those in need.

And my God will supply all your needs according
to His riches in glory in Christ Jesus.
Philippians 4:19 HCSB

Give, and it will be given to you; a good measure—
pressed down, shaken together, and running over—
will be poured into your lap. For with the measure you use,
it will be measured back to you.
Luke 6:38 HCSB

A generous person will be enriched,
and the one who gives a drink of water
will receive water.
Proverbs 11:25 HCSB

day

56

Cheerful givers are the ones God prizes.
God is able to make it up to you
by giving you everything you need and more
so that there will not only be enough
for your own needs but plenty left over
to give joyfully to others.

II Corinthians 9:7-8 TLB

Lord, thank You for blessing me with such abundance.
Remove any fear or selfishness from my heart
so that I will more quickly and generously give.

WHY DO YOU DOUBT?

Have you been there? You stepped out in faith because God led you to, and suddenly you're thinking, *What have I done?! What if I fail?!* Peter climbed out of the boat in full faith, but he did what so many do: he looked at the forceful wind instead of fixing his eyes on Jesus. It is comforting to know that even when you start sinking from the distractions, Jesus is still there to extend His hand and hold you up. Is it time for you to try this "faith step" again? Stay fixed on Jesus!

"Why are you troubled?" He asked them.
"And why do doubts arise in your hearts?
Luke 24:38 HCSB

But let him ask in faith without doubting.
For the doubter is like the surging sea,
driven and tossed by the wind.
James 1:6 HCSB

Let us run with endurance the race that lies before us,
keeping our eyes on Jesus,
the source and perfecter of our faith.
Hebrews 12:1-2

Climbing out of the boat, Peter started walking on the water and came toward Jesus. But when he saw the strength of the wind, he was afraid. And beginning to sink he cried out, "Lord, save me!" Immediately Jesus reached out His hand, caught hold of him and said to him, "You of little faith, why did you doubt?"

Matthew 14:29-31 HCSB

PRAYER:

Father, forgive me for looking at all the "what ifs" around me instead of staying focused on You. Today is a new day. May I be faithful and committed to looking at You and only You.

GOD'S PEACE IS PERFECT

It's an early summer morning, a light fog is rising off the ground, and you slip into a canoe to quietly row across a still, glassy lake. The only sound is the oar pushing through the water and a cardinal bursting forth his morning song. To have this peaceful state in your mind, when a tornado has just landed, is the peace that passes all understanding. This peace is for you—a gift to you from Christ's Holy Spirit. He will keep you in perfect peace, no matter the chaos surrounding you, when you open this gift and hold onto it as your very own.

The result of righteousness will be peace;
the effect of righteousness
will be quiet confidence forever.
Isaiah 32:17 HCSB

Abundant peace belongs to those
who love Your instruction;
nothing makes them stumble.
Psalm 119:165 HCSB

He calms the storm and stills the waves.
Psalm 107:29 TLB

day

58

I am leaving you with a gift—peace of mind and heart! And the peace I give isn't fragile like the peace the world gives. So don't be troubled or afraid.

John 14:27 TLB

PRAYER:

Father, I long to bask in Your peace—it is peace like no other. Drown out all the noise around me and fill me now with Your great peace.

YOU ARE SAVED BY FAITH

If a stranger walked up to you and said, "I have a million dollars to give away. Would you like to have it?" You'd probably say, "What's the catch?! What do I have to do for it?" And the stranger says, "All you have to do is believe it's real and receive it. Nothing more." That would seem too good to be true! Yet, in the same way, Christ, who is no stranger to you, died so that you can have eternal life, and the only requirement is that you believe on His sacrifice and receive His gift of salvation. There's nothing more you have to do. It's that simple.

We are saved by faith in Christ
and not by the good things we do.
Romans 3:28 TLB

How different from this way of faith is the way of law,
which says that a man is saved by obeying every law of God,
without one slip.
Galatians 3:12 TLB

I can have Christ, and become one with him,
no longer counting on being saved by being good enough
or by obeying God's laws, but by trusting Christ to save me.
Philippians 3:8–9 TLB

day 59

You were saved by faith in God,
who treats us much better than we deserve.
This is God's gift to you,
and not anything you have done on your own.
Ephesians 2:8 CEV

PRAYER:

Lord, living in a world where nothing is free—where you gain nothing without working for it—makes it hard to fully grasp that all I have to do is believe on You for my salvation. What a gift!

JESUS'S REST IS THE BEST

Jesus knows . . . He knows the load you carry each day and the fast pace this world works in which to get things done. That's why He offers the gift of rest—in Him. Other people take energy from you. Things around you take your focus from you. But when you go to Jesus, He doesn't take anything—He gives. He puts into your soul the nourishment and peace you need to experience true rest. Go to Him and rest in Him today.

I am at rest in God alone;
my salvation comes from Him.
Psalm 62:1 HCSB

Therefore my heart was glad, and my tongue rejoiced.
Moreover, my flesh will rest in hope.
Acts 2:26 HCSB

For the person who has entered His rest has rested
from his own works, just as God did from His.
Hebrews 4:10 HCSB

day 60

Come to Me, all of you who are weary
and burdened, and I will give you rest.

Matthew 11:28 HCSB

O Lord, I come to You now to turn away
from my worries and cares and rest in You.

GOD PROVIDES FOR EVERY NEED

It's amazing how you can be going along in life and come across this verse to stop you in your tracks. Why? Because of one word—need. If you were to list all of the needs you're asking God to fill, then go back and seriously reevaluate them, chances are that many are actually wants. Yet when you chisel down to the actual needs, they are met. If you're shaking your head no, it could be that what you think you need isn't what you really need—at least not for today. He supplies all your need exactly when He knows you need it.

God gives seed to farmers and provides everyone with food.
He will increase what you have,
so that you can give even more to those in need.
II Corinthians 9:10 CEV

Instruct those who are rich in the present age not to be arrogant or to set their hope on the uncertainty of wealth, but on God, who richly provides us with all things to enjoy.
I Timothy 6:17 HCSB

"Bring to the storehouse a full tenth of what you earn so there will be food in my house. Test me in this," says the LORD All-Powerful. "I will open the windows of heaven for you and pour out all the blessings you need."
Malachi 3:10 NCV

day

61

And my God will supply all your needs according to His riches in glory in Christ Jesus.

Philippians 4:19 NASB

God, I trust You, I trust You, I trust You to provide exactly what I need when I need it. Forgive me for ever doubting You.

ADVENTURE IN GOD'S WORD

Have you ever gotten a treasure map and followed all the clues to find and unearth a trunk of gold coins? Probably not, but it sounds like fun, doesn't it? Well, each day of your life is like a treasure hunt—full of gifts and surprises waiting to be found by you, and God's clues are in the Holy Bible. If you read it every day, searching and hunting for His direction and guidance, you will find treasures of righteousness, knowledge, wisdom, and even God Himself—all that you need in order to fulfill His purpose for you. Don't delay! Open the pages and let the adventure begin!

In the beginning was the Word,
and the Word was with God,
and the Word was God.
John 1:1 NIV

Jesus answered them, "You are deceived,
because you don't know the Scriptures
or the power of God.
Matthew 22:29 HCSB

For God sent Him, and He speaks God's words,
since He gives the Spirit without measure.
John 3:34 HCSB

day 62

All Scripture is inspired by God and is
profitable for teaching, for rebuking,
for correcting, for training in righteousness,
so that the man of God may be complete,
equipped for every good work.
II Timothy 3:16-17 HCSB

Lord, oh how I love Your Word!
It is like a treasure that leads me to golden truths
and fulfills my longing to know You more.
There is none like it.

SET YOUR MIND ABOVE

What does it mean to set your mind on things above? Of course, God and His omnipotence; of course, God's goodness to humankind and to you; and, of course, knowing that you have eternal life with Him. But there's more. When you think on things above, you put your mindset in the heavens with God. When your mindset is fixed on the Creator of the universe, you can look beyond the close-up of today's challenges and remember there is a much bigger purpose at work in your life. Keeping the bigger picture and looking at an even bigger God means peace and satisfaction for your soul. And that is good.

We demolish arguments . . . we take captive
every thought to make it obedient to Christ.
II Corinthians 10:5 NIV

When I look at your heavens, the work of your finger,
the moon and the stars, which you have set in place,
what is man that you are mindful of him.
Psalm 8:3-4 ESV

Behold, I see the heavens opened,
and the Son of Man standing at the right hand of God.
Acts 7:56 ESV

day 63

Set your minds on things above,
not on earthly things.
Colossians 3:2 NIV

Lord, I ascribe to You the glory due Your name, and worship You in the splendor of Your holiness. Compared to You, my source of strength and hope, my worries are ever so small. What a mighty God You are!

GOD'S WAYS ARE NOT OUR WAYS

One of the most important things to remember when making plans—whether for your life or for the day—is to hold those plans loosely. There almost always will be a detour of some kind that means a change of direction, time, course—sometimes even canceling the whole idea! This is because, while you are plotting the easiest way, the Lord is planning the best way for working in you the faith and character He wants to develop. These detours are usually seen as inconveniences and irritants, but they're actually blessings in disguise. Yes, His ways and thoughts are different, but they are always better and come from a place of indescribable love.

Don't boast about tomorrow,
for you don't know what a day might bring.
Proverbs 27:1 HCSB

"For I know the plans I have for you," declares the LORD,
"plans to prosper you and not to harm you,
plans to give you hope and a future."
Jeremiah 29:11 NIV

Many are the plans in a person's heart,
but it is the LORD's purpose that prevails.
Proverbs 19:21 NIV

day

64

"For My thoughts are not your thoughts,
and your ways are not My ways."
This is the LORD's declaration.
Isaiah 55:8 HCSB

Father, it's hard not making my own plans,
but I look to You now and ask what You would
have me to do and where You would have me to go.
I love You and want Your best plans for me.

THE FRUIT OF GOD'S SPIRIT LIVING IN YOU

If love, joy, peace, patience, kindness, goodness, faithfulness, gentleness, and self-control are what you get *after* you receive God's Holy Spirit, what does it mean you had before? No love? No joy? Lack of peace, impatience, ill-will, harshness, no faith, and . . . lack of control? Wow, the thought is pretty sobering and offers something to think about. While any of us without Christ may have had some of these tendencies, even to a small degree, isn't it comforting to know the qualities we have to look forward to as we let the Holy Spirit rule in us each day?

But the one sown on the good ground—
this is one who hears and understands the word,
who does bear fruit and yields: some 100, some 60,
some 30 times what was sown.
Matthew 13:23 HCSB

Therefore produce fruit consistent with repentance.
Luke 3:8 HCSB

We are asking that you may be filled with
the knowledge of His will in all wisdom and spiritual
understanding, so that you may walk worthy of the Lord,
fully pleasing to Him, bearing fruit in every good work
and growing in the knowledge of God.
Colossians 1:9-10 HCSB

day

65

The fruit of the Spirit is love,
joy, peace, patience, kindness,
goodness, faithfulness,
gentleness, self-control.
Galatians 5:22-23 ESV

PRAYER:

Lord, I know I can't live with these qualities without Your help! I pray for Your control over my will so I can display patience, kindness, self-control—all of these—in a way that people see You in me.

PRAISE THE LORD!

When something happens that irritates you, you've probably experienced the struggle to stop thinking about it. There could be a million things you need to do, but all you can do is think about that one thing. And the next thing you know, the entire day has gone by, and you're still focused on it. It's hard to understand why it's so hard to "let it go" and move on to positive thoughts. But there is a quick cure—remember to praise God! Yes, think on anything He has done for you and build your praises from there. That irritant might not vanish altogether, but it will shrink in the shadow of His goodness and grace in your life.

Praise our God, you peoples;
let the sound of His praise be heard.
Psalm 66:8 HCSB

Blessed be the name of God forever and ever,
to whom belong wisdom and might.
Daniel 2:20 ESV

Oh, the depth of the riches both of the wisdom
and the knowledge of God! How unsearchable His judgments
and untraceable His ways!
Romans 11:33 HCSB

Let all that I am praise the LORD;
may I never forget the good things he does for me.

Psalm 103:2 NLT

PRAYER:

Father, I do praise You for countless ways that You have blessed me—from Your provision, Your love, Your faithfulness, Your grace. I could go on and on because You are so good to me.

YOU ARE GIFTED

Wow, that's a lot of gifts! And God has touched down and activated the ones He instilled in *you*. There is so much work to do in your family, your church, your neighborhood and community, and when you embrace your holy gifts for God's work, fasten your seatbelt because mighty things will happen! Most of all, you will experience more divine fulfillment and supernatural strength than you've ever imagined. So . . . what are your gifts? Are you using them for God's kingdom and glory?

Pursue love, and earnestly desire the spiritual gifts,
especially that you may prophesy.
I Corinthians 14:1 ESV

Since you are so anxious to have special gifts from the Holy Spirit,
ask him for the very best, for those that will be
of real help to the whole church.
I Corinthians 14:12 TLB

Each of you should use whatever gift
you have received to serve others,
as faithful stewards of God's grace in its various forms.
I Peter 4:10 NIV

day 67

According to the grace given to us,
we have different gifts: If prophecy,
use it according to the standard of one's faith;
if service, in service; if teaching, in teaching;
if exhorting, in exhortation; giving,
with generosity; leading, with diligence;
showing mercy, with cheerfulness.

Romans 12:6-8 HCSB

PRAYER:

Lord, please give me the faith, confidence,
and trust to embrace my spiritual gifts and to use them for
helping at church and making a difference in my neighborhood.

TOUCHED BY HIS MERCY

When you were a child, was there ever a time when you needed help with something, but you were afraid to ask because you would look silly or stupid? Or, how about as an adult? Childhood fears don't necessarily go away just because you've grown up. Well, this verse lifts the veil of shame, embarrassment, or insecurity and instills complete permission to freely and confidently ask for the help you need. No timidity or indignity allowed—you can boldly share your weaknesses and know that God will reach down and bless you with His mercy and love. He is with you and for you. Always.

Have regard to the prayer of your servant and to his plea,
O LORD my God, listening to the cry and to the prayer
that your servant prays before you this day.
I Kings 8:28 ESV

Answer me when I call, God, who vindicates me.
You freed me from affliction;
be gracious to me and hear my prayer.
Psalm 4:1 HCSB

It happened that while Jesus was praying in a certain place,
after He finished, one of His disciples said to Him,
"Lord, teach us to pray just as John also taught his disciples."
Luke 11:1 AMP

day

68

So let us come boldly to the throne of
our gracious God. There we will receive his mercy,
and we will find grace to help us
when we need it most.

Hebrews 4:16 NLT

PRAYER:

O Lord, I am so glad I can approach Your throne
and call on Your name with confidence! In fact, You like it!
Nothing is too trivial or shameful or embarrassing.
You want to hear about everything. Thank You for this gift.

FORGIVENESS IS FOR YOU

This verse just says it like it is: God won't forgive you unless you forgive others. That sounds heavy, but He doesn't hang this condition on you like a ball and chain—it's to free you. You might be thinking, *But you don't know what he or she did to me!* No, but God knows and He'll deal with it. But the harder you hold on to unforgiveness, the harder your heart gets and squeezes out His healing balm of grace for you. It also blinds you to your own sin, which you need forgiveness for too. It may feel like jumping off a cliff, but forgiveness is a dive worth taking into God's sea of cleansing, simply because He says so. Trust Him in this.

Lord, you are kind and forgiving and
have great love for those who call to you.
Psalm 86:5 NCV

But if you don't forgive people,
your Father will not forgive your wrongdoing.
Matthew 6:15 HCSB

Then Peter came to him and asked,
"Lord, how often should I forgive
someone who sins against me? Seven times?"
Matthew 18:21 NLT

day 69

Remember, the Lord forgave you,
so you must forgive others.
Colossians 3:13 NLT

Okay, Lord, this is not easy, but I love You
and know that You only want the best for me.
So, I will choose forgiveness.
It may be one day at a time, but it's a start.

PRUNED BY THE MASTER GARDENER

Mature grape vines loaded with grapes are a true sign that the vine keeper, or gardener, knows exactly what he's doing. It takes wisdom to know the right soil content, sun exposure, and pruning methods so all the nourishment in the roots makes its way to the vine tips to boost growth within the grapes. Likewise, in a Christian's life, proper soil of the heart, Son exposure, and pruning from life's difficult trials are vital for developing fruits of righteousness and a life that shines in a dark place. So stay close to the Gardener—although at times it's painful. He daily tends your heart and life to reflect His great care for you.

The one who remains in Me and I in him produces much fruit,
because you can do nothing without Me.
John 15:5 HCSB

A man who endures trials is blessed,
because when he passes the test he will receive the crown of life
that God has promised to those who love Him.
James 1:12 HCSB

Every branch in Me that does not bear fruit, He takes away;
and every branch that continues to bear fruit,
He [repeatedly] prunes, so that it will bear
more fruit [even richer and finer fruit].
John 15:2 AMP

day 70

I am the true Vine,
and my Father is the Gardener.
John 15:1 TLB

Lord, I can tell when Your pruning shears are working on me, and it's never pleasant. But I know it's for my good, and I love You for wanting to refine and shape me into a more beautiful person.

WALK BY FAITH

Did you know that, at this very moment, you're moving one thousand miles per hour? For the earth to make a complete rotation in twenty-four hours, it's got to spin that fast. It doesn't feel or look as though you're moving—it feels like you're sitting still—but you are actually *whirling*. This is much like the dailyness of life. You can work hard and pray day after day and not feel as though you're making any progress. But in God's bigger plan, there is a lot of movement, you just can't see it. This is when God stretches your faith and encourages you to keep living with all hope and trusting that He is with you working away to complete the work He has started in you.

Faith is the assurance of things you have hoped for,
the absolute conviction that there are realities
you've never seen.
Hebrews 11:1 VOICE

Above all, taking the shield of faith with which you will
be able to quench all the fiery darts of the wicked one.
Ephesians 6:16 NKJV

For night and day we pray on and on for you,
asking God to let us see you again,
to fill up any little cracks
there may yet be in your faith.
I Thessalonians 3:10 TLB

7

For we walk by faith, not by sight.

II Corinthians 5:7 HCSB

Lord, help me to keep a bigger picture when it comes to my life.
Even when I don't see action or change,
I have faith that You are with me,
working to grow my faith even more.

THE LORD IS NEAR TO YOU

The Lord is near . . . *you*. When you rise each morning and plan out your day, He is near. When you celebrate a mountaintop moment, He is near. When you lie in bed for weeks from illness, He is near. When you rebel and repent, He is near. Whatever you do, wherever you go, He is near—today, tomorrow, for the rest of your life on earth and into eternity. Embrace this promise, remember it always, and never let it go.

The LORD is near the brokenhearted;
He saves those crushed in spirit.
Psalm 34:18 HCSB

Surely His salvation is near to those who fear Him,
so our land will be filled with His glory.
Psalm 85:9 NLT

But now [at this very moment] in Christ Jesus you who once were [so very] far away [from God] have been brought near by the blood of Christ.
Ephesians 2:13 AMP

day 72

The Lord is near.

Philippians 4:5 HCSB

O Lord, I want You near, I need You near all the time. I love Your presence and the comfort it brings and the strength I gain. Thank You for being near to my heart.

SAFE IN GOD'S SHELTER

Have you ever seen a mama duck take her babies out into the wide-open world? It's so cute to watch as she divides her brood and spreads her wings over each group. As they waddle together, her wings cover, hide, steer, shade, and shelter. She knows of dangers her babies don't yet know about. Your heavenly Father's protection is much the same. He covers and hides you from harm, He provides cool relief in the scorching seasons of life, He guides you in the way you should go, and He protects you from the enemy's attempts to harm. He shields you with His wings—it's a promise.

We live within the shadow of the Almighty,
sheltered by the God who is above all gods.
Psalm 91:1 TLB

For you have been a stronghold to the poor,
a stronghold to the needy in his distress,
a shelter from the storm and a shade from the heat.
Isaiah 25:4 ESV

For You have been a shelter for me,
a strong tower from the enemy.
Psalm 61:3 NKJV

day

73

He will shield you with his wings!
They will shelter you.
His faithful promises are your armor.

Psalm 91:4 TLB

PRAYER:

Father, thank You for protecting me the way You do. Because of You, I can feel safe, secure, and confident in all that I do.

amen

JOY IN THE MIDST OF CARES

From what source does your comfort come? A big hug? Hearing the words "I love you"? Curling up in an oversized chair with steaming coffee on a rainy day? These sources are wonderful, and they do bring comfort, yet they touch only the surface of whatever weighs on your heart, and they last only as long as the moment you receive them. But when you call on the Lord and reach for His loving embrace, He pours into you His strength and hope and laces it with deep-rooted joy. Yes, joy in the midst of your cares. It's something only a God of love can do, and He happens to love you.

For as the sufferings of Christ overflow to us,
so through Christ our comfort also overflows.
II Corinthians 1:5 HCSB

Jerusalem, rise from the ruins! Join in the singing.
The LORD has given comfort to his people; He comes to your rescue.
Isaiah 52:9 CEV

Now may our Lord Jesus Christ himself and God our Father,
who loved us and through grace gave us eternal comfort
and good hope, comfort your hearts and strengthen them
in every good work and word.
II Thessalonians 2:16-17 NRSV

day 74

When I am filled with cares,
Your comfort brings me joy.

Psalm 94:19 HCSB

PRAYER:

Dear God of all comfort, I run to You now to receive the deep and lasting comfort only You can give.

CHRIST HAS SET YOU FREE

Imagine being a little bird locked up in a cage only to sit on a perch, never to use your wings. But one day, someone carries your cage outside, lifts the door, and says, "Fly, little one! Fly as God made you to!" Oh, the wonder and excitement, the joy and the rush from that first *push* off the door frame and into the open sky. After flying into freedom, you wouldn't fly back into that cage again . . . or would you? So often that's what we do after God releases us from shame or whatever prison our heart was in before. But freedom in Christ doesn't come with a return address. When He says free, He means *free.*

For the Lord is the Spirit,
and wherever the Spirit of the Lord is, there is freedom.
II Corinthians 3:17 NLT

If you continue in My word, you really are My disciples.
You will know the truth, and the truth will set you free.
John 8:31-32 HCSB

But thanks be to God, that you who were once slaves of sin have become obedient from the heart to the standard of teaching to which you were committed, and, having been set free from sin, have become slaves of righteousness.
Romans 6:17-18 RSV

day

75

Christ has set us free to live a free life.
So take your stand! Never again let anyone
put a harness of slavery on you.

Galatians 5:1 THE MESSAGE

PRAYER:

O God, thank You for setting me free from the weight of sin
I used to carry. My spirit is more alive than ever.
I love my life surrendered to You and You alone.

FAITH, HOPE, AND LOVE

Faith, hope, and love—three golden threads that, when woven together, make a lifeline to God and others that cannot be broken. Wear them around your neck, tie them to your heart, live them openly around others to experience the boldness and grace He gives no matter your circumstance. They are His gifts to you—embrace them wholeheartedly with the fullness of gratitude!

Faith shows the reality of what we hope for;
it is the evidence of things we cannot see.
Hebrews 11:1 NLT

Through him [you] are believer in God,
who raised him from the dead
and gave him glory, so that your faith and hope are in God.
I Peter 1:21 ESV

"Love the Eternal One your God with all your heart
and all your soul and all your mind."
This is the first and greatest commandment.
Matthew 22:37-38 VOICE

day 76

Three things will last forever—
faith, hope, and love—
and the greatest of these is love.

I Corinthians 13:13 NLT

PRAYER:

Lord, it's because of You and Your sacrifice for me
that I am able to love the way that I do.
I love being in love with You.

GOD'S WORD WILL STAND FOREVER

Just how old is the Bible, anyway? The answer's not that simple because it wasn't written all at one time; it was written by forty different authors over a 1,500-year period. The first book was written around 1400 BC, the last book around AD 90. So going back to the first book, the Bible would be over 3,400 years old! And if you counted from when the last book was written, it'd still be over 1,900 years old. Considering the fact that the Bible is the highest selling book to date ever, even after all these centuries of time, it looks obvious that it's going to last forever. Besides, God's own Word says it will, and His Word is truth. What a *gift*!

In the beginning was the Word, and the Word was with God,
and the Word was God. He was with God in the beginning.
John 1:1 NIV

LORD, Your word is forever; it is firmly fixed in heaven.
Psalm 119:89 HCSB

I promise that my Spirit and my words that I give you will
never leave you. They will be with your children
and your grandchildren. They will be with you now and forever.
Isaiah 59:21 ICB

day 77

The grass withers and the flowers fall,
but the word of our God endures forever.

Isaiah 40:8 NIV

Wow, Lord, the thought that I am reading words
that generations have read before me and
will be read by generations after me
is humbling and exciting. I love Your Word!

GOD DELIVERS YOU THROUGH TRIALS

King Darius had just witnessed a miracle: Daniel spent an entire night in a den with wild, hungry lions and walked out unharmed. There is no explanation except that God ruled over the lions' desire to eat Daniel, and the miracle changed a king's life. Are you in a den with lions right now? Is your faith being tested and you're wondering what in the world is going on? Well, God is going on—He is working in you to trust Him more than ever, and displaying for others His presence and goodness. Yes, goodness. Your life is a testimony. It's about others seeing Christ and His power in you so they will want Him too—the way a king was won over through Daniel!

This Jesus the Nazarene was a man pointed out to you
by God with miracles, wonders, and signs that God did
among you through Him.
Acts 2:22 HCSB

The LORD is my rock, my fortress, and the One who rescues me;
My God, my rock and strength
in whom I trust and take refuge.
Psalm 18:2 AMP

[Peter] said, "I am certain that the Lord sent
his angel to rescue me from Herod and from everything
the Jewish leaders planned to do to me."
Acts 12:11 CEV

day 78

He rescues and delivers; He performs signs and wonders in the heavens and on the earth, for He has rescued Daniel from the power of the lions.

Daniel 6:27 HCSB

PRAYER:

Lord, please, help me! Help me have the same unflinching faith in You that Daniel displayed when he stepped into the lions' den!

GOD IS GOOD, SO LET'S GIVE THANKS

Rejoice in the Lord! Give thanks to God! Worship and praise His holy name! Why? For the gift of your very life and those you love; for His never-ending and unfailing love for you. How? In all ways of speaking, singing, praying, loving, and serving. When? This moment, all moments, especially when you least feel like it. Your heart will be made glad! Where? Anywhere and everywhere. Instead of having an "off limits" think of every place you go as "on limits." His faithful love endures forever, so let's let our praise endure forever too!

Every good and perfect gift is from above,
coming down from the Father of the heavenly lights.
James 1:17 NIV

O give thanks to the LORD, call on his name,
make known his deeds among the peoples!
I Chronicles 16:8 RSV

Give thanks to God no matter what circumstances
you find yourself in. (This is God's will
for all of you in Jesus the Anointed.)
I Thessalonians 5:18 VOICE

day 79

Give thanks to the LORD for He is good;
His faithful love endures forever.
Psalm 118:29 HCSB

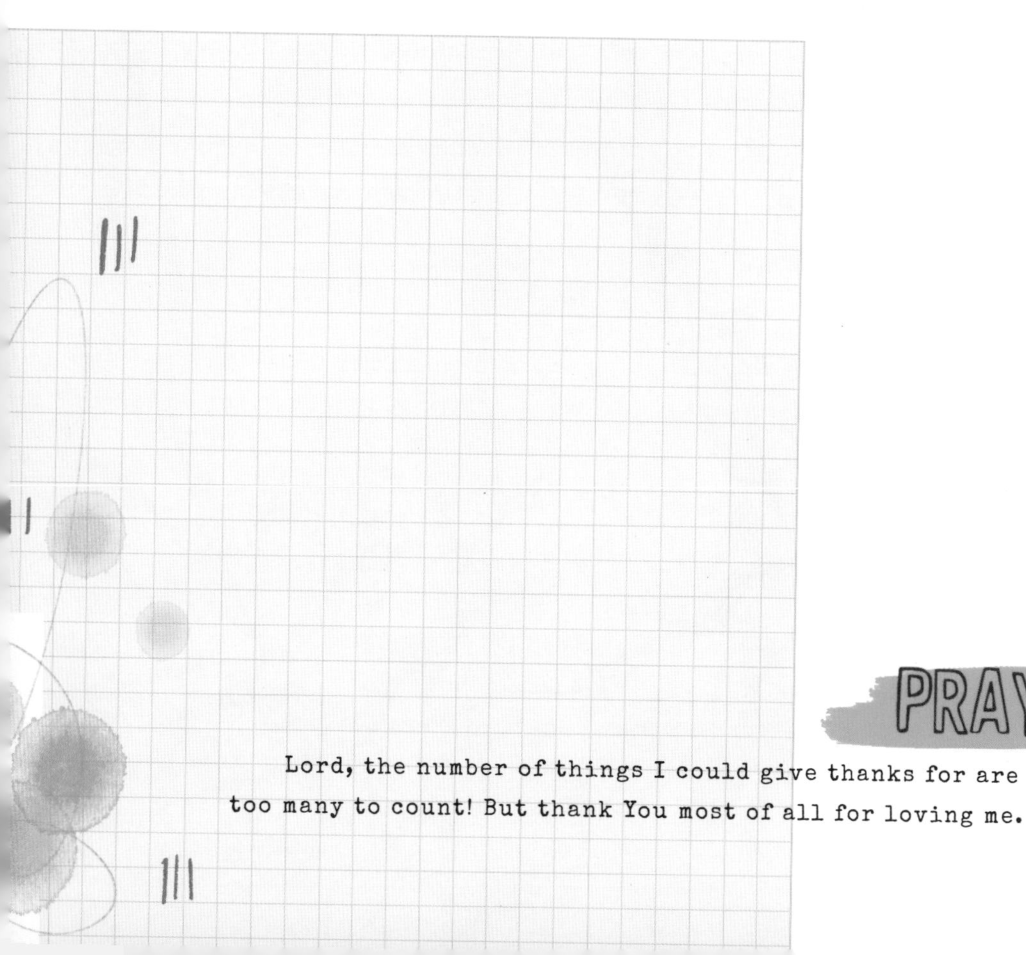

PRAYER:

Lord, the number of things I could give thanks for are too many to count! But thank You most of all for loving me.

GOD WILL GRANT YOU HIS WISDOM

When was the last time you were granted something? Was it last month when you entered a private venue such as a music hall or football stadium? Or maybe it was access to a website meant for golden club members? Well, if you've read your Bible lately, you were granted wisdom from God above! Webster's defines *grant* as "to allow fulfillment of; to bestow or transfer formally." Every time you search the Scriptures with an eager heart, God fulfills, bestows, transfers His wisdom on to *you*! That means He's doing all He can to help you make good choices, grow in His favor, and simply experience His presence. There is nothing *unwise* about that!

If any of you lacks wisdom, let him ask God,
who gives generously to all without reproach,
and it will be given him.
James 1:5 ESV

For to the man who is pleasing in His sight,
He gives wisdom, knowledge, and joy.
Ecclesiastes 2:26 HCSB

The Eternal, Commander of heavenly armies,
is the source of such wisdom. His advice is wonderful.
Isaiah 28:29 VOICE

80

For the Lord grants wisdom! His every word is
a treasure of knowledge and understanding.
Proverbs 2:6 TLB

Father, with so many decisions
to make coming from all different directions,
I need wisdom—Your wisdom—because I know it's the best,
most sound help I could ever receive.

HELP IS THERE—JUST ASK!

When you're running low on physical strength, all you've got to do these days is grab an energy drink and protein bar and you're set. But what about when you need inner strength and even some courage to go with it? You can have the strongest muscles and be fit enough to run a marathon, but if you don't have the mental and spiritual capacity to face a challenge, you're toast! The good news is, God's got you covered. All you need to do is ask. He's ready and waiting this very moment to hear your voice, to empower you, and to embolden you in exactly the ways you need.

But when you pray, go into your room, close the door and
pray to your Father, who is unseen. Then your Father,
who sees what is done in secret, will reward you.
Matthew 6:6 NIV

Answer me when I call, O God of my righteousness!
You have relieved me in my distress;
Be gracious to me and hear my prayer.
Psalm 4:1 NASB

I will call upon the LORD, who is worthy to be praised;
so shall I be saved from my enemies.
II Samuel 22:4 NKJV

day 81

As soon as I pray, you answer me;
you encourage me by giving me strength.

Psalm 138:3 NLT

PRAYER:

Lord, I need You. Please give me the strength
I need to do the work You've given me to do today.

PERFECT HOPE, PERFECT PEACE

Hope is . . . believing for what you do not see. Sometimes it's easy to have hope because everything is moving straight toward the finish line of your dream—that's happy hope. Other times, circumstances look so bleak, there is little hope left—or waning hope. But, when you trust in the God of hope and not in the results of what is hoped for, you can have hope overflowing with peace and joy because the outcome is in His perfect hands. That's holy hope. He is the One true source of perfect hope and perfect peace.

Lord, when doubts fill my mind, when my heart is in turmoil,
quiet me and give me renewed hope and cheer.
Psalm 94:19 TLB

So don't lose hope. I, the LORD, have spoken.
Jeremiah 31:17 CEV

But since we belong to the day, we must be serious
and put the armor of faith and love on our chests,
and put on a helmet of the hope of salvation.
I Thessalonians 5:8 HCSB

day 82

Now may the God of hope fill you
with all joy and peace as you believe in Him
so that you may overflow with hope
by the power of the Holy Spirit.
Romans 15:13 HCSB

Dear Lord, my hope is in You and no other,
because You are a loving and holy God.

YOUR BIGGEST CHEERLEADER

One of the most unsettling things to go through in any job is the dreaded "annual evaluation." Ugh. It's a time when you and your supervisor rate your progress from the previous year and state your goals for the upcoming one. If the feedback isn't positive, it's easy to get frustrated and work in fear of getting demoted, even fired. But in God's economy, there is freedom in knowing He never gives up on you. He knows you're not perfect and will make mistakes, but He has a plan for your life, and He won't abandon that plan or you. He will show up every day rooting you on, helping you to accomplish more than you could have ever imagined. Now that's a good God!

My grace is sufficient for you,
for power is perfected in weakness.
II Corinthians 12:9 HCSB

I am with you always, to the very end of the age.
Matthew 28:20 NIV

Now glory be to God, who by his mighty power at work within us
is able to do far more than we would ever dare to ask
or even dream of—infinitely beyond
our highest prayers, desires, thoughts, or hopes.
Ephesians 3:20 TLB

day 83

And I am certain that God,
who began the good work within you,
will continue his work until
it is finally finished on the day
when Christ Jesus returns.
Philippians 1:6 NLT

Lord, thank You for knowing my heart and seeing how hard I try. Mostly, thank You for always being here to help me every day. I love You.

DON'T BE ANXIOUS ABOUT TOMORROW

A mind full of thoughts can be hard to rein in. One minute they can spin around about what to have for breakfast and before you know it, they've catapulted into how you're going to pay next month's bills or if you'll be in the next round of layoffs at work. When this happens, one anxiety adds to another and . . . panic attack! Since none of us knows what tomorrow really holds, spending time and energy focused on the unknown is futile and exhausting. Plus, when looking at tomorrow, you miss out on the simple pleasures of today. So rest in today, give thanks for the present moment, and believe that God has already got your tomorrow under control, because . . . He does.

Jesus said to His disciples, "For this reason I tell you,
do not worry about your life, as to what you will eat;
or about your body, as to what you will wear."
Luke 12:22 AMP

God, examine me and know my heart;
test me and know my anxious thoughts.
Psalm 139:23 NCV

May Your faithful love rest on us, Yahweh,
for we put our hope in You.
Psalm 33:22 HCSB

day 84

So don't be anxious about tomorrow.
God will take care of your tomorrow too.
Live one day at a time.
Matthew 6:34 TLB

Lord, I want Your peace. Please take from me the troubles on my mind and fill me with Your presence and peace.

HIS PRESENCE, HIS COMFORT

When going through a deep valley in life, it's easy to feel lost because your mind gets dark and muddled. It's hard to know where to go or what to do next. But just as a shepherd leads and protects his sheep, your heavenly Father does the same for you. Sheep get excited and stressed over very small things, but when they feel their shepherd's rod constantly touching their shoulder, leading and letting them know he is there, they remain calm and secure. You too can feel safe and at peace—He is with you always.

My presence will go with you,
and I will give you rest.
Exodus 33:14 HCSB

But you have upheld me because of my integrity,
and set me in your presence forever.
Psalm 41:12 ESV

The LORD is near the brokenhearted;
He saves those crushed in spirit.
Psalm 34:18 HCSB

day 85

Even when I go through the darkest valley,
I fear no danger, for You are with me;
Your rod and Your staff—they comfort me.
Psalm 23:4 HCSB

Lord, thank You for Your presence
and comfort no matter the time or place.
Knowing You are with me
helps my spirit to rest.

GOD IS YOUR FRIEND

You can have a lot of friends, but there are very few with whom you can share your deepest thoughts. Your bond can be so tight, you know what the other is thinking or how she'll react in any given situation. Did you know that, in the same way, God is your friend—the closest you'll ever have? He loves your company and wants to hear what is on your heart and share what He knows will bless yours. It's true—He really does. Won't you call to Him now?

And I say to you, My friends,
don't fear those who kill the body,
and after that can do nothing more.
Luke 12:4 HCSB

Then she called the name of the LORD who spoke to her,
"You are God Who Sees."
Genesis 16:13 AMP

Why am I praying like this?
Because I know you will answer me, O God!
Psalm 17:6 TLB

day 86

Call to me and I will answer you.
I'll tell you marvelous and wondrous things
that you could never figure out on your own.
Jeremiah 33:3 THE MESSAGE

PRAYER:

Lord, I want to hear from You! I call to You now and share from the depths of my heart. Then I will be silent and wait to hear Your voice.

ARE YOU THINKING OUTSIDE THE BOX?

You've probably heard the term "think outside the box." Well, God's been thinking and performing miracles outside everyone's box for thousands of years! From parting the waters of the Red Sea, to feeding over five thousand people with five loaves of bread and two fish, to bringing Lazarus back to life and resurrecting Jesus from the grave—God has been and still is going above and beyond anything we can possibly imagine. So, what is it that you need, or what dream or vision do you have that you've no idea how it will come about? Through the power at work in you through God's Holy Spirit, ask Him now!

God All-Powerful has done great things for me,
and his name is holy.
Luke 1:49 CEV

I will stretch out My hand and strike Egypt with
all My miracles that I will perform in it.
After that, he will let you go.
Exodus 3:20 HCSB

I am pleased to tell you about the miracles
and wonders the Most High God has done for me.
Daniel 4:2 HCSB

day 87

Now to Him who is able to do above
and beyond all that we ask or think according
to the power that works in us.
Ephesians 3:20 HCSB

O God, I know that You are a God of miracles,
yesterday and today. I trust in You to hear my prayer and
by Your Spirit accomplish Your will in my life!

HOPE IS AN ANCHOR

Have you ever tried to lift an anchor? They are heavy! Their weight is determined by the size of the vessel they're meant to hold during high current and wind conditions. No matter how harsh the weather, the boat it's attached to will stay securely in place until weather calms and returns to normal. Likewise, the hope you have in God is stronger than the very trial you are facing so you won't be moved. Through hope, you are anchored to Him who will never let you go and who will supply all help as you rest in Him.

"The LORD is my portion and my inheritance,"
says my soul; "therefore I have hope in Him
and wait expectantly for Him."
Lamentations 3:24 AMP

Always fear the LORD.
For then you will have a future,
and your hope will never fade.
Proverbs 23:17–18 HCSB

Let us hold unswervingly to the hope we profess,
for he who promised is faithful.
Hebrews 10:23 NIV

day

88

We have this hope as an anchor
for our lives, safe and secure.
Hebrews 6:19 HCSB

Father, no matter what is going on around me,
no matter how bleak my situation seems,
I will cling to the hope I have in You. You are faithful!

HEALING FOR YOUR HEART

Our God is not an idle God. He looks deep into your heart and searches for soft spots that are bruised so He can instill a touch of His love and healing. If you need encouragement, He brings it through a friend who texts that she's praying for you. If you need compassion, He gives it through a hug from a coworker in the next cubicle. If you need prayer, Jesus Himself prays on your behalf to the Father according to His will for you. So when those weak and downcast heart moments come, soak in the comfort that waits just for you.

Now God has revealed these things to us by the Spirit,
for the Spirit searches everything, even the depths of God.
I Corinthians 2:10 HCSB

Search me, O God, and know my heart!
Try me and know my thoughts!
Psalm 139:23 ESV

Christ Jesus is the One who died,
but even more, has been raised;
He also is at the right hand of God
and intercedes for us.
Romans 8:34 HCSB

day 89

And He who searches the hearts knows
the Spirit's mind-set, because
He intercedes for the saints according
to the will of God.

Romans 8:27 HCSB

PRAYER:

Jesus, I imagine You know my heart and more about what I need than I do. Thank You for the comfort that comes from knowing You are with Me and praying to the Father on my behalf!

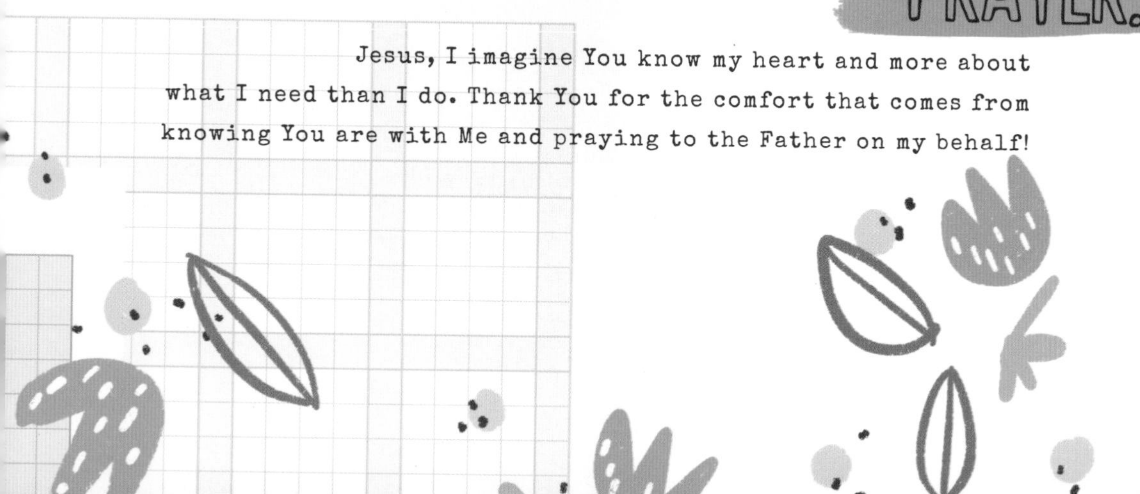

GOD'S WAY IS THE BEST WAY

Parents, teachers, mentors—they all have one thing in common: they inform and guide so that you will learn. But also, they want to protect you from making the same mistakes they've made. Yet isn't it interesting that oftentimes you still want to try something the way *you* think it should be done regardless of any warning? That's the human spirit for you! Well, God's Word is God-breathed, and with all the instruction—and warning—through kings, queens, prophets, apostles, disciples, and Jesus Himself, why wouldn't you want to read it before making decisions? God's way is the best way. Always.

Be strong and brave. Be sure to obey all the teachings
my servant Moses gave you. If you follow them exactly,
you will be successful in everything you do.
Joshua 1:7 NCV

I have hidden your word in my heart
that I might not sin against you.
Psalm 119:11 NIV

For their advice is a beam of light directed
into the dark corners of your mind to warn you of danger
and to give you a good life.
Proverbs 6:23 TLB

day 90

Now, my children, listen to me,
because those who follow my ways are happy.
Listen to my teaching, and you will be wise;
do not ignore it.
Proverbs 8:32–33 NCV

Lord, forgive me for the times I haven't turned to Your Word before solving a problem. I do believe Your Word is truth and will look to it more for wisdom and direction.

GOD SO LOVED THE WORLD . . .

There is no greater love than to lay down your life for someone. It means making the other person more important than yourself, even if it means death to you and your dreams. Throughout history, people who've died while protecting others are considered heroes. No words can describe the depth of sacrifice heroes make, whether for one person or several. Yet, Jesus laid down His life for all of humanity so that we can have the hope of eternal life with Him. That includes you. He died for you. There is no greater act of love.

This saying is trustworthy and deserving of full acceptance:
"Christ Jesus came into the world to save sinners"—
and I am the worst of them.
I Timothy 1:15 HCSB

Only Jesus has the power to save! His name is the only one
in all the world that can save anyone.
Acts 4:12 CEV

For I am not ashamed of the gospel, for it is the power of God
for salvation to everyone who believes, to the Jew first
and also to the Greek.
Romans 1:16 ESV

day 91

For God loved the world in this way:
He gave His One and Only Son,
so that everyone who believes in Him
will not perish but have eternal life.

John 3:16 HCSB

Jesus, thank You from the depths of my heart for loving me so much that You died for me. I am so grateful and can't wait to see You face to face in all Your beautiful glory.

NO CONDEMNATION IN CHRIST

BAM! slams the gavel. "Guilty as charged!" says the judge. "In order to make restitution for your wrongs, you will go to prison!" he orders. That's what happens when someone commits a crime. Well, we all qualify for standing in front of God and awaiting the consequences of our life marked with sin. Except, when you have Jesus, God won't slam a gavel and condemn you for anything, especially not to a prison cell. No, instead He appoints His Son, Jesus, to serve the time for you. Jesus has saved you—all of us—from living under the condemnation of law. That is love.

But the LORD will redeem those who serve him.
No one who takes refuge in him will be condemned.
Psalm 34:22 NLT

Therefore, as one trespass led to condemnation for all men,
so one act of righteousness leads to justification
and life for all men.
Romans 5:18 ESV

If the ministry that brought condemnation was glorious,
how much more glorious is the ministry
that brings righteousness!
II Corinthians 3:9 NIV

day 92

God did not send his Son into the world
to condemn it, but to save it.

John 3:17 TLB

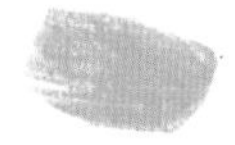

Jesus, thank You for taking away the weight of judgment and condemnation from my heart! Thank You for making me free!

HE IS WITH YOU

Ever enter a building, look up, and see yourself on a minicam? Somewhere there is a hidden lens watching your every move so that if you do something wrong, there's no question about what you did or how you did it. In the opposite way, when you love the Lord and look to Him as your source of hope and provision, He sees every move and hears every heartfelt prayer of love expressed toward Him. Even if it doesn't feel like it, He is with you—throughout each frenzied day and every toss-filled night, watching and listening for your cries. He is with you, and He will help you.

He brought me out into a spacious place;
he rescued me because he delighted in me.
Psalm 18:19 NIV

He is before all things,
and by Him all things hold together.
Colossians 1:17 HCSB

For the LORD watches over the way of the righteous.
Psalm 1:6 HCSB

day 93

Watch this: God's eye is on those who respect him, the ones who are looking for his love. He's ready to come to their rescue in bad times; in lean times he keeps body and soul together.

Psalm 33:18 THE MESSAGE

PRAYER:

Lord, I love You. I am so grateful and comforted that You are with me and watching over me, ready to help at my beck and call.

BEAUTY FOR ASHES

Earthquakes, hurricanes, wildfires—the destruction caused by these events can be absolutely shattering to the victims left in their wake. There are also internal catastrophes that rupture the places of the heart, wiping out all traces of hope and strength to survive. Both situations stun the soul into a place of mourning. When all is quiet and words don't come, is God there? The answer is . . . yes. He's not only there, He is working as only He can to revive and rebuild the ashes into beautiful pillars, the spirit of grief into a garment of praise. He is there, He is still God, and His glory remains forever.

Jesus was going all over Galilee, teaching in their synagogues,
preaching the good news of the kingdom,
and healing every disease and sickness among the people.
Matthew 4:23 HCSB

If my people will humble themselves and pray, and search for me,
and turn from their wicked ways, I will hear them from heaven
and forgive their sins and heal their land.
II Chronicles 7:14 TLB

As He stepped ashore, He saw a huge crowd,
felt compassion for them, and healed their sick.
Matthew 14:14 HCSB

day 94

To all who mourn in Israel he will give:
beauty for ashes; joy instead of mourning;
praise instead of heaviness.
For God has planted them like strong and
graceful oaks for his own glory.

Isaiah 61:3 TLB

PRAYER:

Father, I trust You are here . . . with me now.
I sink into Your loving arms and rest in Your embrace.

GOD LEADS THE WAY

If you ever looked at God's resume, you'd see that since the beginning of time, He's led His people in the way they should go. He led the Israelites out of Egypt with pillars of cloud, He led Shadrach, Meshach, and Abednego through a fiery furnace, and He led Joseph and Mary to a stable in time for Jesus's birth. He still leads today using methods that are exactly the way that ministers to your heart. His leading isn't always pleasant—it could be through a rejection letter or in closing doors on a business—but when you trust the closed doors as much as you do the opened ones, His joy and fulfillment can be yours, no matter where He leads.

He renews my life;
He leads me along the right paths
for His name's sake.
Psalm 23:3 HCSB

With your unfailing love you lead the people you have redeemed.
In your might, you guide them to your sacred home.
Exodus 15:13 NLT

The Spirit shows what is true and will come
and guide you into the full truth.
John 16:13 CEV

day 95

This God, our God forever and ever—
He will always lead us.

Psalm 48:14 HCSB

PRAYER:

Father, make me ever so sensitive to Your leading, and keep my heart willing to go, because I trust that You know what and where is best for me.

A DAY OF REST

The thought of working a Monday through Friday job and having the weekend "off" sounds ideal, doesn't it? But aren't weekends spent running around doing errands? And what about the kids and their activities?! Having the weekend off often makes you glad to go back to work on Monday! Well, even though observing the Sabbath is an Old Testament law, your body, mind, and spirit still need rest. God created the Sabbath not only for your rest, but for His worship. As you worship Him, He pours His power, strength, and refreshment right into you for the next round of busy days ahead. So take care of you—make a day of rest so you can be your best.

[Jesus] said to them, "Come away by yourselves
to a remote place and rest for a while."
Mark 6:31 HCSB

He lets me rest in green meadows;
he leads me beside peaceful streams.
Psalm 23:2 NLT

Anyone who enters God's rest will rest from his work as God did.
Hebrews 4:10 NCV

day

96

The Sabbath was made for man.
Mark 2:27 HCSB

Lord God, I need rest—Your rest. I worship and praise You from my heart. And by Your grace, I receive a spirit of renewal to help me do the work You've given me to do this day and the next.

HE MAKES YOUR HEART CLEAN

When you think back on your childhood days at school, you probably have memories of your teacher picking up an eraser and erasing all the writings and drawings from the day before off the chalk board. When he or she got done, the slate was clean to write new material for that day's lesson. Well, when you confess and turn from ways you know are not pleasing to God, He wipes the heaviness from those ways so the slate of your heart becomes clean—literally. His forgiveness is instant and brings a lightness and joy that can come from no other source. It's His promise to you. Sound good? Go on, give it a try!

But you were washed, you were sanctified,
you were justified in the name of the Lord Jesus Christ
and by the Spirit of our God.
I Corinthians 6:11 ESV

If we confess our sins, He is faithful and righteous to forgive us
our sins and to cleanse us from all unrighteousness.
I John 1:9 NASB

He saw Jesus, fell facedown, and begged Him: "Lord, if You are
willing, You can make me clean." Reaching out His hand,
He touched him, saying, "I am willing; be made clean."
Luke 5:12-13 HCSB

day 97

Repent and turn back, so that your sins
may be wiped out, that seasons of refreshing
may come from the presence of the Lord.
Acts 3:19 HCSB

Lord, I want Your lightness and joy! I come to You now and share from my heart what I know is not right, and receive Your gift of forgiveness. Thank You for loving me. I love You too.

YOU ARE SAVED BY GRACE

You are saved by grace! What a relief, don't you think? That means there is no amount of good works or reward points to earn your way into eternal life. Besides, if you did have to work your way, how much work would be enough? None! No, you are saved as soon as you believe on God's Son and accept Him into your heart. Your faith in Him ignites His holy grace as your stamped pass into His presence for eternity. This way, God gets all the glory—He alone sits on the throne of the universe. Praise Him!

The law indeed was given through Moses;
grace and truth came through Jesus Christ.
John 1:17 NRSV

But because of his great love for us, God, who is rich in mercy,
made us alive with Christ even when we were dead
in transgressions—it is by grace you have been saved.
Ephesians 2:4–5 NIV

Let all the world look to me for salvation!
For I am God; there is no other.
Isaiah 45:22 TLB

day 98

For you are saved by grace through faith,
and this is not from yourselves; it is God's gift—
not from works, so that no one can boast.
Ephesians 2:8-9 HCSB

Jesus, what a gift! My heart overflows with thanksgiving
that I can live in the covering of Your grace.

GOD IS A CONSTANT SOURCE

With life so full of various trials and burdens to bear, it's easy to feel as though you're on the verge of breaking down or having the rug pulled out from under you at any moment of any given day. That's why there's tremendous comfort and security in knowing that you aren't alone and that God is not only a source of stability, He is a constant source. He doesn't pour from His pitcher and run out of Himself; His flow of love, solidity, safety, and wisdom are of an endless supply! He doesn't ration these gifts between you and others—you can draw all that you need and want without holding back.

The LORD is my rock, my fortress and my deliverer;
my God is my rock, in whom I take refuge,
my shield and the horn of my salvation, my stronghold.
Psalm 18:2 NIV

Reverence for God gives a man deep strength;
his children have a place of refuge and security.
Proverbs 14:26 TLB

So I tell you, you are Peter. And I will build my church on this rock. The power of death will not be able to defeat my church.
Matthew 16:18 ICB

day 99

He will be the sure foundation for your times,
a rich store of salvation and wisdom and knowledge;
the fear of the LORD is the key to this treasure.
Isaiah 33:6 NIV

Thank You, Father, for being a steady rock on which to hold when circumstances are so unpredictable. I draw from You this very moment for wisdom to know what to do and strength to do it.

GOD'S PROMISES ARE FOR YOUR LIFETIME

God didn't create you and bring you into this world to fend for yourself. He gives breath, hope, and closeness with Him throughout every moment of every day. And for your journey, His promises are just that—promises. He gives His Word as a lifeline to knowing His thoughts and ways on how to live so that you have a good life and one that glorifies Him. He is your Helper and Protector, Redeemer and Savior, and through Him you have everlasting life. All praise and glory to Him!

Every word of God is flawless;
he is a shield to those who take refuge in him.
Proverbs 30:5 NIV

I will sing of the steadfast love of the LORD, forever;
with my mouth I will make known your faithfulness
to all generations.
Psalm 89:1 ESV

For as many as are the promises of God,
in Christ they are [all answered] "Yes."
So through Him we say our "Amen" to the glory of God.
II Corinthians 1:20 AMP

day 100

Because of his glory and excellence,
he has given us great and precious promises.
These are the promises that enable you
to share his divine nature and escape
the world's corruption caused by human desires.
II Peter 1:4 NLT

PRAYER:

Lord, Your promises are truth and light for me! I rejoice that I can claim each and every one for myself and my life. You are almighty, You are love, and I praise You from my heart for Your goodness to me and all humankind.

About the Author

Shanna Noel lives in Washington State with her husband of eighteen years, Jonathan, and their two daughters, Jaden (15) and Addison (10). When they aren't covered in paint and Bible journaling, they are working on reclaimed projects around the house or catching up on the latest movie.

Shanna is the founder and owner of *Illustrated Faith* and the Bible-journaling community, and stands in awe at what God is doing in their creative community!

Dear Friend,

This book was prayerfully crafted with you, the reader, in mind—every word, every sentence, every page—was thoughtfully written, designed, and packaged to encourage you . . . right where you are this very moment. At DaySpring, our vision is to see every person experience the life-changing message of God's love. So, as we worked through rough drafts, design changes, edits, and details, we prayed for you to deeply experience His unfailing love, indescribable peace, and pure joy. It is our sincere hope that through these Truth-filled pages your heart will be blessed, knowing that God cares about you—your desires and disappointments, your challenges and dreams.

He knows. He cares. He loves you unconditionally.

BLESSINGS!
THE DAYSPRING BOOK TEAM